What a Young Woman Should Know About Sex

WHAT A YOUNG WOMAN SHOULD KNOW ABOUT SEX

REVISED EDITION

Answers to Personal Problems

by *John F. Knight, M.B.B.S.* *

*A standard medical degree in British countries

PACIFIC PRESS PUBLISHING ASSOCIATION
Mountain View, California
Omaha, Nebraska   Oshawa, Ontario

Cover by D. Tank; other color photos by E. W. Were
Cover design by Lauren Smith

Contents

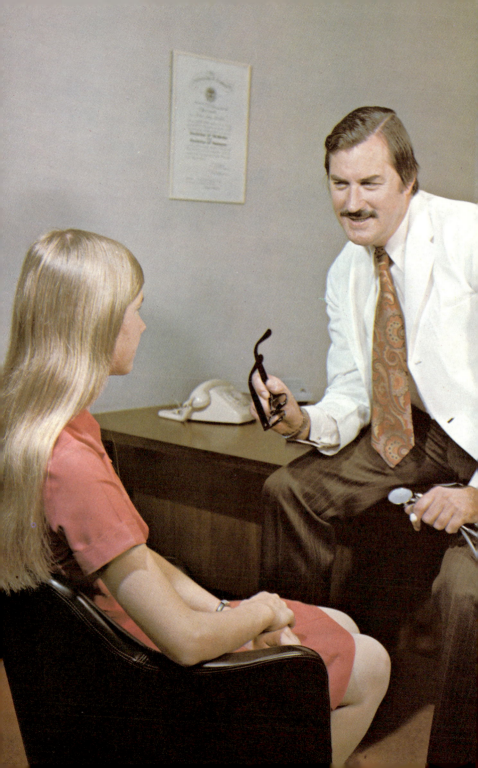

Let's Get Acquainted!

Hi!

Good afternoon!

I hear they've asked you to write a book.

Yes.

So that's why you asked me to come around.

Precisely. I need your help.

But I don't write books. I don't even write.

So what? I still need your assistance. You see, this book is going to be different.

Something new under the sun?

Not altogether. There's nothing new under the sun. There are only different angles.

Tell me. What's the big new line?

Simply this. I've got a special "thing" about kids. I happen to like them. Not long ago we were kids ourselves. In a few years' time today's youngsters will be parents, leaders, the professionals of the upcoming era.

Agreed.

Every generation, however, seems to be a jump or two ahead of the previous one. In other words, youth is racing ahead at a progressively greater speed all the time—physically, mentally, emotionally. You name it, they're there. Or rather, they *were* there. By the time you've caught up, they've almost outpaced you!

Amazing, isn't it!

Certainly. But you know, despite this tremendous surge forward in general knowledge, I often make some startling discoveries.

Ohhhh! You mean our computer-age offspring aren't quite as "with it" as we believe?

In a sense, yes. No doubt their knowledge of many things is extensive, and far outweighs that of their counterparts of twenty or thirty years ago. But very often this knowledge is quite superficial. Many have a smattering of information covering a wide range of topics. But when it comes down to basics, there is frequently a terrible scarcity of sound, reliable information.

What makes you so sure of this? After all, you could be wrong!

I could be wrong, I agree. But I don't think so. You see, I've been using a rather reliable set of yardsticks over the past few years. I've used these to discover just what the upcoming generation is thinking about; in short, what makes them tick.

Tell me more. What are these yardsticks you're talking about?

There are three of them, all told. Number one is purely good luck. I like to tell my friends it is due to good management, but that wouldn't be true.

You see, we have four children ourselves. Girl-boy-girl-boy. Just like that! Right now they're in this wonderful age group we plan to talk about. Being father (and question answerer) to four modern young people whose minds are jam-packed with every conceivable query keeps a person up with the way the current teen-age mind works.

After all, the queries I'm asked are merely a compilation of their own thinking plus the summarized, computerized total of what their friends think as well.

What their friends think is again a total of what *their* friends, acquaintances, reading habits, and so on, produce. This, I believe, is the most reliable "feedback" information system available.

OK. Now what is the second yardstick you use?

I sit in my office for many hours each day and listen to people. I hear every aspect of living. I listen in on problems of life, problems of living, the problems of youth (the range covers everything from the discreet to the indiscreet).

It doesn't take long to build up an appreciation of what fills the average teen-age mind. You soon appreciate the problems that loom as giant-size ogres. You learn of weaknesses, inner conflicts, doubts, fears. You soon realize how much and how little the youthful mind comprehends the basics of life.

Interesting. Now yardstick number three?

To me, this is perhaps the most enlightening. In many respects it is the most rewarding.

As you know, I regularly write several magazine and newspaper columns that are medically oriented. These have a very wide circulation. They are quite straightforward and deal with the simple basics of good health.

However, the interesting reaction is what regularly happens as a result of these columns, articles, and booklets.

What does happen?

They collectively generate an enormous mail. People write from far and wide. Problems, problems, problems!

Many letters reach my desk regularly, mostly from the younger set, but of course the entire age range is represented.

Everyone merely writes: "Dear Doctor—"

They do not know who I am, and I do not know them. Therefore, they feel free to express their views, their hidden fears, and outline their most intimate problems. I am staggered at the frankness that many of my unseen, unknown correspondents exhibit.

But I fully believe that this represents life at its basic best. The overwhelming number of questions are serious, thoughtful, perplexing. They represent king-sized bogies that are worrying the writer. Otherwise they would not expend the effort of putting pen to paper.

How interesting!

Interesting it is. But what is more interesting in my opinion is the relentless frequency with which certain aspects of life are dealt with.

Correspondents living thousands of miles apart will write letters which are virtually identical.

When it comes to the teen-age group, the frequency of repetition multiplies at an astounding rate.

In fact, so frequent are many queries that we've printed special replies to cope with the means of replying to them!

I have absolutely no doubt that this is a true reflection of what youngsters are thinking. Piece by piece you can sum up what is in the mind of the average person who is growing up. To my way of thinking, this is an invaluable yardstick. It measures the "pulse" of youthful reaction, thought, doubt, questioning.

You mean, it gives you a kind of uncanny insight?

Precisely.

So that is to form the basis of this book?

In a sense, yes. I believe lots of books have been written in years past without the writers really having a true insight into how their readers are thinking. Why write material if it's redundant before it's printed? Why produce material that's out of date with the current thinking of your reading audience? It's a waste of time, waste of effort, waste of money.

This, then, will answer every young person's prayer?

Not exactly. But we'll do our best to provide answers to the most commonly asked questions of the present-day upcoming generation. We're taking the lid off growing youth, you might say.

So it's a modern-day version of the "birds and the bees" story?

Today we assume that the majority of youngsters are well informed about the birds and the bees (often inaccurately, but the basics are usually pretty straight) by the time they leave primary school. We certainly do not intend to preach kid's stuff to people with a reasonable basic knowledge of what goes on in this world. But we do want to get the record straight. We hope to present the facts of life, along with related aspects.

So that's what this book is all about?

In essence, yes. As you and I talk together, we hope to cover pretty well every aspect of life that is important to growing youth. There will be gaps, for sure. Some parts will appear overemphasized. Some will appear ridiculously simple. But don't forget, what may appear basic and commonplace to one reader may not be very familiar to another person living in some other totally different environment. In short, we're doing our best, and are being guided by the questions that continually pour into our office. There must be some guiding influence. We believe that this is the best one yet invented.

Great. Now let's get along with chapter two. What did you say we needed to start talking about?

2

What Makes Teen-agers Tick?

What are little girls made of?

Sugar and spice and all things nice. That's what little girls are made of!

I learned that at school. I'm sure nobody believes this anymore. Not in these sophisticated days!

You're right. Little girls are certainly great. I love every square inch of them all. But we're out to discuss bigger girls.

Like the teen-age variety?

Certainly. In brief, we want to talk about growing youth. Let's say the age range from twelve to the twenties—"the stormy teens," as one person put it. A tremendous number of changes take place in this wonderful age segment. It's the time when a little girl leaves all that behind. It's the period in which she emerges from a child and gracefully develops into adult womanhood.

It's a tremendous time segment. It is also a very significant one.

Dramatic changes take place inside the system as the "new you" suddenly blossoms forth.

It's the time of development. Physically, mentally, and

spiritually the body takes on new functions, adopts new roles, takes on different appearances.

Mentally there are significant advances. The desires, whims, attitudes of early childhood are swept aside. These are replaced by sensible, mature thought. Reasoning starts to play an important part in daily living. In short, the little girl becomes a woman.

And how can you account for this sudden, tremendous upsurge of internal activity?

This is no easy question to answer. We tend to put it all down to "nature." It just happens that way! It's supposed to, so it does. Just as the flowers start to grow and blossom every spring, so the human being suddenly surges forward to growth and beauty at a certain stage of life.

Basically and briefly, what takes place inside the system at the onset of all this vigorous activity?

All manner of things. But before we discuss the changes, let's give a brief rundown on normal anatomy and physiology. It's only by having a reasonable working knowledge of what the inner apparatus consists of that alterations to this can be described and fully appreciated.

Let's start with the normal female reproductive system then.

Right. The starting point is pretty obvious. The female genital tract is called the vagina. This canal is four to six inches long, commencing at the exterior, and extending upward and inward.

The entrance is guarded by two folds of tissue. The larger outer one is call the labia majora, and the inner smaller one is termed the labia minora. In simple terms, large lips and small lips.

These extend across to the midline and afford protection to the sensitive tissue with which the canal is lined.

Above, where the smaller lips unite, there is a tiny organ called the clitoris. It is loaded with ultrasensitive nerve endings. Under certain circumstances, which we'll describe more fully later on, it can be the source of marital pleasure. The entire concept of becoming married, lovemaking, and producing children are in fact closely related to the attributes of this organ.

Where do we go from here?

The external entrance is technically referred to as the introitus. You know, physicians prefer to have their own vocabulary. It sounds much more dignified when discussing intimate parts to use the faceless mechanics of words which are meaningless to those not in the know. It allows doctors to view with impartial detachment parts which are guarded with modesty by the population in general. We'll let you know the various technical terms. But we'll keep their subsequent use to a minimum, and preferably use only the more commonly known ones. We don't want this book for teen-age girls to become a weighty textbook!

Where does the "hymen" fit into the picture?

The hymen is a thin membrane that sometimes completely or partially covers the introitus (vaginal entry).

Once upon a time, in fact until only recent times, special significance was often attributed to the hymen. But today opinions and views are radically altering. The fragile membrane is seen as a purely developmental remnant. It is very easily broken. It is indeed unusual to discover a fully intact one when examining a patient, whatever the age.

Very occasionally it completely covers the entry. But more often, only a fragile rim remains at the portal of entry.

Today, increasing interest and participation in sports by Miss Modern and the almost universal use of internal tampons from earliest menstruation collectively break down what remains of the tissue of the hymen.

It was believed in days gone by that an intact hymen was guarantee of a girl's virginity. In fact, some European countries still cling to the old idea.

A few years ago I used to have large numbers of Europeans as patients. Like anyone else, they had their share of internal pelvic problems. But I noted with interest a great reluctance on their part (or rather on the part of the parents of the patients) for them to undergo a normal pelvic examination. Indeed, a pelvic operation was often regarded with abject horror by them.

If any pelvic surgery was necessary (and indeed even after simple pelvic examinations), the parents frequently demanded a medical certificate outlining the reasons why this was carried out, actual dates, findings, and so on!

To us this all seemed quite unnecessary, and indeed a bit ludicrous. However, they apparently still clung to the idea that anything penetrating the canal would break down the thin hymenous membrane and for all practical purposes end the young lady's state of "virginity."

Just what degree of premarital explanation goes on with an aspiring spouse I have never been able to discover. But it is all so unnecessary and indeed misleading to rely on this as an indication of "purity."

Does the hymen ever play an important part in normal development though?

In rare instances, where it completely covers the introitus, it can interfere with menstruation. In effect, it can seal off the entrance, or conversely, the "exit" for menstrual blood flow.

Where this occasionally occurs, it most likely comes to medical attention when normal menstruation fails to occur in a girl who normally should have commenced her periods. A simple pelvic check will soon indicate the problem.

What happens?

Instead of the usual entrance, a bulging membrane is seen obviously sealing off the area. It bulges because the vaginal canal is packed with the blood from successive menstruations.

How is this treated?

Very simply. The thin membrane is incised, the blood

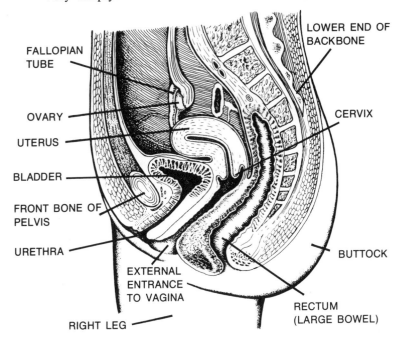

FALLOPIAN TUBE

LOWER END OF BACKBONE

OVARY

CERVIX

UTERUS

BLADDER

FRONT BONE OF PELVIS

URETHRA

BUTTOCK

EXTERNAL ENTRANCE TO VAGINA

RECTUM (LARGE BOWEL)

RIGHT LEG

THE FEMALE PELVIS

This is a section through the female pelvis, and the chief organs of reproduction are being viewed from the left side.

The vaginal canal sits between the canal from the bladder, called the urethra (in front), and the part of the bowel called the rectum. At the upper end the uterus juts into the vagina. On either side of the uterus lie the Fallopian tubes, and the ovaries are located at the far end of each tube.

released, and the patency (as we call it) of the entrance restored, or rather established.

Could we hurry on? We're really digressing a bit from our basic plan. If you recall, we're dealing with the basic anatomy of the female pelvic organs.

True. But a few interesting digressions should help to press home general points here and there.

We've dealt with the external anatomy. Now what about the inside areas?

Just near the entry to the vagina are several glands. These have an important function. They are really specialized little factories.

That's a strange place for a factory. What is the function?

Under nervous excitation they produce a special fluid. Basically this is a lubricating material. At certain times a copious volume of thickish fluid will ooze from the ducts of these glands. Basically it's aimed at making intercourse simple and friction-free. All manner of strange things can occur here, but we'll talk about this later on as well. Once more, it's a case of noting the presence of these glands.

What about the canal itself?

This is lined with a delicate membrane which is quite sensitive. Normally, it is taut and elastic-walled, and a multiplicity of ridges crisscross its entire surface. Also it contains many tiny glands embedded in the lining, and these produce fluids under nervous stimulation.

Where does the "womb" fit into the picture?

At the far end of the canal the womb (technically called the uterus) juts down into the canal.

The womb is a smallish organ, roughly the size and shape of a pear. The narrow end is called the cervix, or neck. The larger, roundish portion is called the corpus, or body, of the uterus.

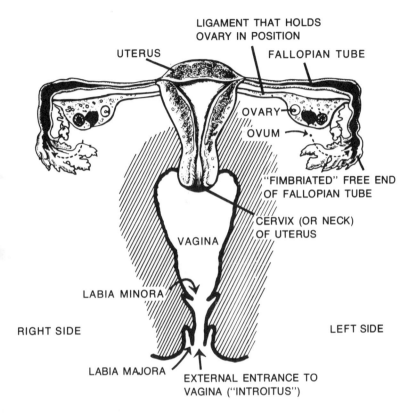

LIGAMENT THAT HOLDS
OVARY IN POSITION

UTERUS

FALLOPIAN TUBE

OVARY

OVUM

"FIMBRIATED" FREE END
OF FALLOPIAN TUBE

CERVIX (OR NECK)
OF UTERUS

VAGINA

LABIA MINORA

RIGHT SIDE

LEFT SIDE

LABIA MAJORA

EXTERNAL ENTRANCE TO
VAGINA ("INTROITUS")

FEMALE ORGANS OF REPRODUCTION

This is a diagrammatic view of the female reproductive organs as they are located when viewed directly from the front. (Compare this picture with the "Sectional" one on a previous page.)

Once more it shows the continuity of the pathway from the exterior into the vagina, up into the womb (uterus) via the cervical canal, then out into the Fallopian tubes at the uppermost corners of the uterus. At the far end of the tubes are "fimbriated" tentacles that are in close relationship to the ovaries where the microscopic eggs (ova) are produced.

On the left side, an ovum has just been released by the ovary, and the dotted line shows the track it will follow. The free waving tentacles of the tube help sweep the ovum into the tube itself.

Pregnancy may occur in the tube if a male cell is encountered here.

In actual fact, the cervix forms the upper part of the vaginal canal. During a pelvic examination, it's possible to view the cervix under direct vision. It is seen as a semispherical object jutting into the upper part of the vagina. In the center of the rounded part is a small aperture. This is called the external os, or simply the outer hole. Actually the cervix is a very important part of the body.

Isn't this where cancer so often strikes in later life?

True. In fact, women seem to be unlucky. It's estimated that cancer of the cervix is one of the commonest sites for this deadly disease in the female.

Can you see a cancer when you look at the cervix?

In advanced cases you certainly can. But in early stages it is often quite impossible. Frequently it is the site for ulcers and discharging sores. Left untreated, these may smolder on. A certain proportion of these can become malignant (cancerous) later on if left.

Isn't this the part involved with the popular Pap smear?

Yes. A thin "smear" of cells is removed from the cervix by a special instrument the physician uses. These are subsequently examined under the microscope by the pathologist. He can tell almost at once if any sinister malignant cells are present. This way you'll have either a "positive" or "negative" smear test.

Doesn't the contour of the cervix change during life?

It varies enormously. In younger women who have not carried a baby it is usually elongated and tends to come to a rounded conical-shaped blunt end.

However, after a first pregnancy the shape varies a good deal. The conical appearance disappears. It becomes flatter and wider. It is usually fairly simple to tell if a woman has carried a baby or not, merely by examining her cervix.

Tell us something about the rest of the uterus.

The remainder of the womb is this pear-shaped muscular organ. It has a small cavity inside. The cavity is lined by special tissue called endometrium. Sorry, there is no simple term for this one. You'll just have to remember the word.

Under normal circumstances the cavity is quite narrow. Indeed, the sides are in apposition. Entrance to the cavity is via the small external os we mentioned earlier.

The external os leads into the cervical canal. This is a short canal that passes along the neck of the uterus. Where it ends internally is termed the internal os. This immediately opens out into the cavity of the uterus itself.

Where do the "tubes" and "ovaries" fit into the picture?

Internally, the upper part of the cavity of the womb widens out into two horns called cornua. These are directly linked with the fallopian tubes, one on the right and the other on the left-hand side.

The tubes are about four inches long. They are narrow structures, and as their name implies are "tubes" in the full sense. They are lined internally with special cells, each containing hairlike projections called cilia.

Under normal circumstances the cilia move at a regular rate and a wave of motion occurs, being directed toward the womb.

Anything contained in the tube tends to be propelled automatically toward the womb. In fact, each month just after ovulation (the time when the female egg is shed from the ovary), this microscopic object enters the far end of the tube and is energetically swept along toward the uterus.

At the far end of the tube is a strange-looking ending termed the fimbriated part of the tube. Fingerlike projections of tissue extend out. It is believed that they play a part in catching the egg each month after its release and in helping steer it into the entrance of the tube.

Aren't the ovaries connected to the tubes somehow?

Closely related to the far end of the tube on each side sit the ovaries. These are whitish, almond-shaped organs which measure 3.8 cm (1.5 in) by 1.9 cm (.75 in). They are held in place by special ligaments.

The ovaries are tremendously important for many years of life. They serve a twofold function. First one or the other produces a tiny egg each month. Second, they produce potent chemicals called hormones. These play a tremendous part in the normal menstrual cycle and in a woman's becoming pregnant. Besides all this, ovarian hormones are essential to normal female development. They help form the typical "curves" that we associate with the female body.

Hormones also play a key part in the way women feel. They have a tricky way of "kicking back" on the nervous system. They are responsible, directly and indirectly, for arousing emotions, arousing and settling tempers, putting "pep" into the system and a spring into the step. We'll tell you more about these high-powered products later on. But as an initial word of caution: Never, never underestimate the power of your hormones!

Are women born with just so many eggs on hand, or can they keep on manufacturing more as time goes on?

At birth, every baby girl has just so many primitive eggs in her ovaries. It has been estimated that these number between 250,000 and 500,000! (Tremendous thought, isn't it? Especially when you contemplate that one egg potentially equals another new life!)

As age advances, many of these die off. But by the time puberty is reached (the time when reproduction becomes possible), between 100,000 and 200,000 eggs (or ova) still remain.

Even this represents a staggering total number.

There are approximately thirty years of reproductive life available to the average woman. Even allowing for no pregnancies, only 300 to 400 of these eggs will ever be shed. So nature has abundantly provided a superabundance of potential eggs.

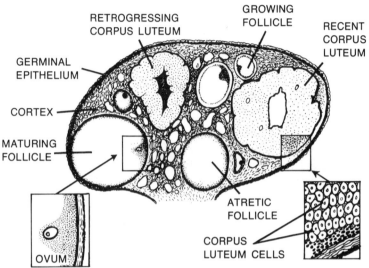

THE WONDERFUL OVARY

Incredible activity occurs within the ovary, and the above composite diagram shows the various phases leading from the formation of an egg (or ovum) to the situations immediately following its release.

The ovary houses thousands of potential eggs, called primordial follicles. Each month one develops, or matures. As it does so, it gradually enlarges, and comes near to the surface of the ovary. The tiny egg itself is finally released from the surface of the ovary and finds its way into a fallopian tube.

The space left by the ovum fills in and is then known as the corpus luteum. This then becomes an important hormone-producing structure.

With the passage of time, the corpus luteum becomes smaller and smaller and finally ceases to produce any hormone at all. Then, little by little, another primordial follicle commences to enlarge and to produce a subsequent ovum.

There are between 100,000 and 200,000 potential eggs in each ovary—or maybe more. The reproductive potential of the ovaries is enormous.

Why do you think nature has been so kind?

A key function of nature is to maintain the regeneration of life. Every effort seems to be directed to this end. Therefore, no chances have been taken. Even under the strangest circumstances, there are still usually plenty of potential eggs to guarantee regeneration of the species.

Supposing one ovary was lost through disease or some other reason, this would still leave a copious number of eggs. In some instances of pelvic disease, it is necessary to remove one ovary, and maybe a large portion of the second one. But ovulation (regular release of the egg) will still take place each month from the remaining part!

Do you think there is any basic significance to all this?

In my simple set of books, I believe there is. As a Christian doctor, I believe the Bible. In Genesis 1, verses 27 and 28, it says: "So God created man in his own image, in the image of God created he him; male and female created he them. And God blessed them, and God said unto them, Be fruitful, and multiply, and replenish the earth."

Just to make certain this early command would be carried out, God implanted in every woman the potential for carrying out this instruction.

A little later on, we shall see He endowed the male with similar attributes.

3

Your Computerized Chemical Factory

Computers are the in thing at the moment. I believe they're growing in numbers and use every day all over the world.

True enough. But I'm sure lots of people (even the computer people, no doubt) don't realize the best-ever computers are the ones we each have been given. For free too!

Sounds interesting. Tell me more.

Our entire systems are basically computer systems. Every day we automatically program in a few basic details. And presto! Out rattle a terrifying series of results.

Usually we're quite unaware of what's going on. It all takes place silently, without commotion, smoothly, and efficiently. In fact, it keeps us alive! Just imagine how we'd get on if we had to remember to breathe so many times each minute. Or if we had to make sure the heart pumped at so many times each sixty seconds! It makes the mind boggle with the terrible consequences that would inevitably result. There is little doubt that the human race would perish in no time! But, fortunately, the automatic processes take over from the moment we are born. The activities inside us vary according to the changing needs of the moment. If we need more oxygen (say from running or working hard), a reprogramming takes place without a hitch. We merely breathe more rapidly and more deeply. The heart beats a little faster, so propelling more blood (and life-giving oxygen) to all parts that need it. It's an incredible arrangement.

Now tell us more about the "chemical factory" we each house.

This is part of the inner computer system too. For a certain number of years the particular plant we're interested in seems to lie dormant. It does virtually nothing.

But suddenly one bright day a little light must come on, and the machinery starts to run. The time for a vital "reprogram" has arrived. Nobody is quite certain what triggers the mechanism off. But it happens with unfailing regularity in the life of everyone.

Is this the time that is called puberty?

Yes. These internal changes can commence anywhere from ten to fourteen years of age. In women, they culminate in the menarche, the time when the first menstrual period occurs.

The menarche usually takes place at the age of thirteen, fourteen or fifteen years. But it is quite variable. In actual fact, it can occur anywhere from ten to fifteen years.

Does menstruation become regular as soon as the menarche takes place?

Sometimes yes, but more often no. I'm glad you brought this question up, for it seems to cause manifold problems with thousands of girls. Every day my mailbag contains letters from girls who are worried stiff because their periods are irregular.

This is nothing to be alarmed about. It may often take many months—and indeed sometimes even years—before the true feminine menstrual system becomes established.

A developing woman hates to be different from her friends. If her best friends commence regular menstruation at the age of twelve, she will feel totally unhappy and even deprived of something if the same has not happened to her at the same age! It's all so ridiculous when viewed objectively. But it's an entirely different situation if *you* are the person so involved.

I've had girls come along whose cycles have not become established as late as seventeen years. Several women patients I see right now have only three to four periods a year. The variations are enormous.

But wide variations such as this surely are not normal?

They are not normal, but often even after full investigation, if no abnormality can be discovered, or just reason for the delays found, one cannot label them "abnormal" either.

I believe the final proof is what finally occurs. After all, the menstrual system is designed for reproduction. If this ultimately occurs, that's proof positive that all is apparently well.

In fact, in each of the instances mentioned above, the young ladies have married. Each now has chalked up two pregnancies, and one is on the merry-go-round for the third time. She still has only three menstrual periods per year— that is, when she is not pregnant!

What actually takes place when menstruation becomes established?

A very interesting, highly complex train of events sets in. It's incredible how accurately the system proceeds. It keeps going in the same pattern for the next thirty years. This represents the active potential productive years of the average woman's life.

Commencing in the ten- to fifteen-year age segment, it proceeds without a break.

Finally, between the average ages of forty-five and fifty

FERTILIZATION TAKES PLACE
AND PREGNANCY OCCURS
(Ovum becomes embedded in lining of uterus)

Corpus Luteum
Continues to
Produce Hormone

Developing
Fetus of
Pregnancy

Embedding

Corpus Luteum Degenerates
if Pregnancy
Does Not Occur

Corpus Luteum
Forms
in Ovary

Discharged
or Normal
Menstruation

Uterus

Tubes

Egg Released

Developing
Ovum

ACTIVITY
IN OVARY

ACTIVITY OF
LINING OF
WOMB
(ENDOMETRIUM)

MENSTRUAL
DAYS

24 28 4 8 12 16 20 24 28 4 8 12 16 20 24 28 4 8 12 16 20 24 28 20 24 28 4 8 12 16 20 24 28 4 8 12 16 20 24

Menstruation   Ovulation   Menstruation   Ovulation   Menstruation   Ovulation   Fertilization   Amenorrhea   Placentation
(no bleeding)

M1   M2   M3

O1   O2   O3

years, it gives up. The so-called change of life (or menopause) sets in, and future reproduction becomes impossible. ("What a relief!" most overworked mothers say with a sigh.)

Can we start with the ovary and find out what happens here?

Toward the end of a normal menstrual period any one of the tiny eggs embedded in the ovary wriggles into life. Remember we told you earlier that there are between 100,000 and 200,000 of these ready and waiting to take off. Technically they are referred to as primordial follicles.

One gradually increases in size and starts to move toward the surface of the ovary. Day after day, under the influence of chemicals called hormones, it increases further in diameter.

Suddenly, about the thirteenth to seventeenth day from the

OVULATION AND MENSTRUATION

This series of diagrams shows the relationship between ovulation and the menstrual cycle over three successive menstrual months.

The state of the ovary is seen in the little diagrams in the upper part of the picture. The state of the endometrium, or lining of the womb, is seen in the lower part.

The dark bands labeled M1, M2, M3 indicate that menstruation is taking place. At this time the unfertilized ovum, together with the inner lining of the womb (endometrium), is shed from the womb entirely. It lasts from three to six days.

The figures under the diagrams indicate the menstrual days (day 1 = the day menstruation commences, ie, when period bleeding starts.)

Soon after menstruation, the lining of the womb commences to build up again, just in case pregnancy occurs. During this time a primordial follicle in the ovary matures. About the fourteenth day it ruptures and leaves the ovary to enter the tube. This day is called "ovulation."

The space where the ovum was located in the ovary becomes the corpus luteum, and produces a hormone that further builds up the lining of the womb. But if pregnancy has not occurred about the twenty-eighth day, the lining (and unwanted ovum) is shed in another normal period bleed.

The entire process repeats monthly.

However, if fertilization occurs (right-hand side of diagram), the fertilized egg becomes firmly embedded in the endometrial lining of the uterus, and pregnancy is under way. The lining becomes very thick, and a copious blood supply is established. This month the lining is not shed as previously. The uterine lining at this point becomes the "placenta" later on.

start of the last menstrual period, the microscopic egg is finally released from the surface of the ovary.

There is a minor explosion, and it simply breaks loose. It is suddenly tossed out into the general pelvic cavity. It never fails to amaze me how the egg is not lost in the great space which surrounds it. It somehow reminds me of the encapsulated astronauts hurtling through space. But just as the computers back home at control center are directing the fate of the capsule, so nature's inbuilt computers are regulating the course of the microscopic ovum.

Fortunately, the gradual buildup of the egg has also seen the development of other aspects aimed at caring for it. The system's hormones which caused it to develop have simultaneously prepared many other parts of the body to receive the ovum. The fingerlike tentacles of the fallopian tubes are ready and waiting to exert a part in steering the egg into the free end of the tube.

Once inside (and rarely is there a miss), the special ciliated cells lining the tubes are at peak performance. Their little hairlike brushes enthusiastically sweep the egg onward and forward. The final objective is the interior of the womb itself.

Isn't it somewhere in the tubes that pregnancy can take place?

Yes. If en route from ovary to womb the egg encounters a male cell, a magical union suddenly takes place. The two cells suddenly merge, forming one brand-new unit. At this moment conception has taken place. Usually it occurs toward the outer segment of the tube.

Is this the only time in the entire month that a woman may fall pregnant?

Yes. It never ceases to amaze me that in the entire menstrual month such a short space of time is available for the occurrence of pregnancy. It takes an ovum a few days to traverse the fallopian tube and arrive at the womb. The time varies a great deal from person to person. But it is a very limited time segment in the overall picture. The actual release of the egg from the ovary is called ovulation. If a male cell is encountered in the tube and union occurs, this is termed fertilization.

Suppose fertilization takes place, what then?

The fertilized ovum merrily progresses on its way and arrives at the uterus (womb). Each month the womb anticipates receiving a fertilized ovum. In the overwhelming majority of months, of course, this does not occur. However, the lining of the womb (which we told you earlier is called the endometrium) has really gone wild. It has become thick and filled with blood vessels. Special cells have developed over the preceding two weeks. All is in readiness to receive the fertilized egg.

As soon as the fertilized egg reaches the lining, it becomes implanted into this prepared area. At that moment a normal pregnancy becomes established.

Further marked changes take place, and nine months later this leads to the birth of a brand-new life.

It's as simple (and as complex) as that!

Now what happens if the egg fails to become fertilized?

A completely different set of circumstances takes place. The egg is propelled along to the womb. But it suddenly finds that nobody wants it any longer.

Suddenly the body regards it as an intruder. A foreigner. Therefore, out. Out, out, out! The womb lining rejects it, spurns it, turns a cold shoulder. It finds no welcome party to encompass and embrace it. In fact, the rich blood supply that has been making the endometrium such a cozy place suddenly freezes up. The blood supply cuts back.

Approximately fourteen days from the moment ovulation

occurs, a gentle shedding of the uterine lining commences.

This gradually increases in force. From a practical point of view, the process we call menstruation takes place. Little by little over the next several days the endometrium is broken down, and bleeding takes place. The egg is shed along with this blood.

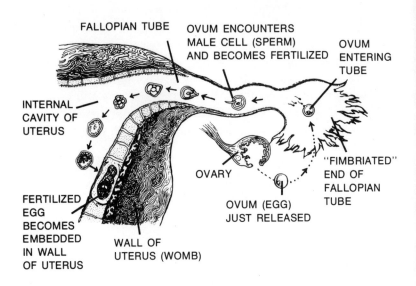

FALLOPIAN TUBE   OVUM ENCOUNTERS MALE CELL (SPERM) AND BECOMES FERTILIZED   OVUM ENTERING TUBE

INTERNAL CAVITY OF UTERUS

"FIMBRIATED" END OF FALLOPIAN TUBE

OVARY

FERTILIZED EGG BECOMES EMBEDDED IN WALL OF UTERUS

OVUM (EGG) JUST RELEASED

WALL OF UTERUS (WOMB)

WHEN "OVULATION" OCCURS

This shows diagrammatically what happens at "ovulation," the time when the microscopic egg (ovum) is released by the ovary where it is manufactured.

Immediately it is released and is swept toward the fingerlike ends of the fallopian tube. These assist the egg to enter the free end of the tube. Here special "ciliated epithelium" lining cells (which contain waving hairlike structures), plus normal movements of the tube wall, help propel the egg along its length.

Fertilization can occur in the tube if a male cell is encountered here. The egg (whether fertilized or not) proceeds along the tube until it reaches the womb (uterus). A fertilized egg becomes embedded immediately in the wall of the womb. But if this has not occurred, the egg plus the lining of the womb is shed, and a normal menstrual period occurs.

After four or five days the bleeding settles down and stops. Back in the "egg factory" another primordial follicle starts to perk up and jumps to life. Once more nature is having a try to reproduce. Will it succeed or won't it? Time alone will tell.

Now what about some more detail on these mysterious chemicals you refer to as hormones?

They are tremendously important and play a key role in life for many, many years. The female has her particular set of hormones. The male has his specific set.

The ovaries, besides producing an egg each month, also manufacture hormones. There are two different sorts. One is called estradiol. This is poured out at a fairly regular rate all through the menstrual cycle. Indeed, it is the presence of this chemical in the system that produces profound changes. It causes the lining of the womb to build up in the early part of the cycle so that it will be receptive to the fertilized egg should conception take place.

Another vital hormone is called progesterone. The tiny space left in the ovary when the egg is discharged each month suddenly fills with fluid. It then becomes known as a corpus luteum. Very quickly this body commences to produce the potent hormone progesterone. For the fourteen days following ovulation progesterone is poured forth. Its aims are many and varied. An important one is to further prepare the lining of the womb for reception of the fertilized egg.

However, if pregnancy fails to take place, its production rapidly ceases. This is quickly followed by the withdrawal bleeding of menstruation.

These two hormones play a vital part on the reproductive system.

Don't they also have something to do with the development of the body at puberty?

Yes, certainly. Under their combined influence, during the

years of puberty, the typical secondary sex characteristics of the individual develop.

What are these?

There is gradual development of the breasts. Up until this time the nipple has been a small, almost unnoticed object. Suddenly, under the direct influence of the sex hormones, small ducts grow inward from the nipples. At the same time the area increases in size. Fat connective tissue is laid down, and milk glands gradually develop.

Aren't there many other features as well?

Several typical feminine features appear. There is a redistribution of the fat deposits of the body. These give the typically female shape and contours to the body in general.

Hair develops in the armpits and in the pubic area.

At the same time there is development of the internal organs of reproduction. The vagina increases in size, and the lining develops. The womb enlarges. Further tissue is laid down to make it a solid organ capable of standing up to the rigors of reproduction.

Earlier you spoke of psychological changes also.

These are vital. A different outlook usually encompasses the entire being. Lots of teen-agers become high-strung—others morbid and depressed. Mental development and the well-known ups and downs of teen-age life get under way.

Would you say, then, there's a reasonable "physiological" excuse for the odd way lots of teen-age girls behave?

It certainly explains why the bizarre actions take place as they often do. But it cannot and should not be used as a blanket excuse for every act of stupidity or absolute irresponsibility.

Lots of growing teen-agers "blame their hormones" for this and that. Everything and anything, from a bad temper to gross negligence, from lack of interest in their normal duties to absolute promiscuity, is often attributed to the poor old hormonal system.

Of course it's fine to have a scapegoat to blame for everything that goes wrong. But remember you are still master of your own system, by and large. You can still exercise conscious control over the majority of your actions. It's a pretty lame excuse, really.

This is a vital time of character building. Basics that are established in this time segment are likely to stick with you for the rest of your life. Give in easily to problems and seek an easy "out" now and you'll be avoiding the issues for years to come.

Take hold of the situation (any situation) right now with both hands, determine to rule it rather than let it rule you, and you've a fighting chance of really making the grade in this rough-and-tumble world.

Are there any other hormones that play a part in all this?

Yes. Many hormones in fact have a finger in the pie. A small gland that sits under the brain (called the pituitary) produces important chemicals as well. These, in fact, are the ones that start the egg cells on their way before they mature into fully formed ova. It also causes the corpus luteum to form.

Still others occur and help the developing fetus (later the infant baby) to form, and remain intact.

One of these is called by the long tongue-twister name chorionic gonadotrophin. It is produced by the placenta, the large piece of material whereby the fetus is attached to the wall of the womb during development. (This later becomes the afterbirth when the baby is ultimately born.)

A certain amount of chorionic gonadotrophin is excreted in the urine of the pregnant mother. Indeed, it is this fact which enables us to carry out the very valuable "pregnancy test'' early in pregnancy when there is still doubt as to whether or not conception has actually occurred.

Later on, another chemical called prolactin is produced. This works on the breast tissue. It actually initiates the flow of milk shortly after the baby has been born.

So there we are. A valuable set of chemicals is being constantly produced in the female system. Most of them have a wide range of functions. They are all important. They are powerful, and often their full potential is underestimated.

But we'll tell you more of those aspects a little further on.

Monthly Problem Time

If you listen to enough girls you'll soon realize that their lives are crowded with problems. Or so it seems. Many of these appear to be related to their regular menstrual cycle.

How true! Not only do we find large numbers of teen-agers (and even those in later age groups) visiting doctors for this reason, but my mailbag, too, is invariably loaded with problems of this nature.

What's the most common problem?

Pains about the time menstruation is due would be the number one contender, but there are plenty of others. Irritability and general mental depression at the same time are quite frequent as well. Lots of girls complain of breast tenderness. The nipples especially seem to become very sensitive, and anything touching this part can cause marked irritation.

Do these symptoms go by any particular name tag? Just about everything–but everything–in medicine seems to have a particular name these days.

Certainly. The majority of symptoms related to menstruation have the blanket term dysmenorrhea.

The symptoms are variable and multiple. Some women breeze through this time of the month, every month, with no problems at all.

I must make it quite clear that this is the usual way it goes. In fact, some researchers recently produced an interesting set of statistics. From a carefully compiled series of records they found that 78 percent of schoolgirls have "no-problem" periods.

However, it's often the minority that is the most vocal. (Isn't this true in every facet of life?)

Of the remaining 22 percent, the breakdown went like this:

17 percent experienced "slight discomfort."

2 percent suffered "subacute" pain.

3 percent encountered "disabling" discomfort.

The general yardstick for measurement was absence either from school or from normal working duties. Further, a check was made if the patient went to bed and, if so, for how long.

These figures are considered to be pretty accurate.

How severe is the pain experienced, and where does it usually strike?

The degree of pain varies enormously. The average girl can toss off the problem with an aspirin and a hot drink and relegate it to the back of her mind. But I have seen others in genuine distress. Indeed, one eighteen-year-old visits me regularly each month. There is no doubt whatsoever that her pain is for real. Normal walking becomes impossible. She describes the discomfort in her back, thighs, and even in the lower pelvic area. She has an ashen color, with perspiring. At times vomiting and prostration take place. Headaches, nausea, constipation, frequency of or difficulty in passing urine may also be common features in extreme cases.

Unlucky victims often describe the pain as "cramplike." It may strike suddenly and severely. Then it may wane a little, only to be replaced by a similar attack soon after. A general sick feeling and mental depression are common with this group. Sometimes dysmenorrhea begins soon after menstruation commences. But more commonly it starts a few years later.

Has anyone discovered the cause for this?

The old idea was that an obstruction or blockage occurred to the normal menstrual flow somewhere in the cervical canal.

Some attributed it to a narrow canal or to a stenosed os—in simple terms a very tiny pinhole-sized opening that was inadequate to cope with the sudden volume of blood trying to escape. But it has since been shown that in most of these women no such situation exists.

But we often hear of simple operations being carried out for this complaint, and in fact, relieving the symptoms.

True. But I doubt if a "dilatation and curette" (as this operation is termed) is done very often merely for this single symptom. All surgical operations carry a risk factor. There is usually some other reason as well before surgery is undertaken.

However, it is quite significant that many of these symptoms vanish like the morning mists following either the operation or a pregnancy. Produce one baby, and your dysmenorrhea will disappear, as I've been admonishing fainthearted damsels for a number of years.

Are there any obvious conditions that you feel could be corrected and so offer these girls some relief?

I believe there are. It is quite significant that dysmenorrhea is frequently associated with a change in routine. A girl lives a happy, gay, relatively carefree sort of life. She attends school. She plays tennis or some other game a few times each week. Maybe she exercises a lot each day, every day.

Perhaps she walks to and from school and has lots of activity during recess and lunchtime.

There is an abundance of fresh air. Vitality is her ever-present partner. There is time for meditation and thought (whether she is aware of it or not, and invariably she is not). But it's present just the same. Mental activity and mental relaxation go along hand in hand.

But one day, sudden change takes place. She is elevated to a higher grade. Or she enters college or university. Or she embarks upon a paid job. Whatever, her simple routine of yesterday suddenly alters radically.

And this produces "disaster unlimited"?

For sure. The degree of exercise is most probably chopped back severely. Instead of playing games several times a week, she is now lucky to get a few hours of mild exercise a week. Often the opportunity disappears entirely.

Often the short periods at her school desk are replaced by long hours at another desk. It may be the benches of a university, or in an office or carrying out routine sedentary duties.

Without the stimulus of fresh air and exercise, the appetite may suddenly plummet. Constipation can set in and become firmly established.

With less exercise she probably drinks less fluid. This further aggravates normal body regularity.

Often there is mental tension—the fear of not passing exams, of not getting assignments in on time, of meeting deadlines, whether at work or at higher educational levels.

If menstrual pain has been experienced, there is always the nagging fear that it will happen again. This may be disastrous if it falls at a key time, such as exams or centered on some important occasion.

This all tends to breed further problems. Somehow, there

is a delicate connection between the brain, the hormonal system, and the womb itself. They are all finely interconnected. It is very easy for trouble to loom up suddenly out of the misty unknown. However, all the foregoing thoughts have been proved to play a part. It is quite significant that if a girl is suddenly transferred from her new problem-crammed environment back to the simple life of yesteryear, her problems (and dysmenorrhea) often suddenly disappear!

Do you have some simple thoughts on treatment for girls with monthly problems?

I certainly have. First, go for the simple, free, inexpensive lines of therapy. They often work. They are worth a trial run every time.

Stick to a simple, all-round diet each day. One high in protein and vitamins is essential. This builds without fattening. It keeps the system in tip-top condition.

Personally, I go for a vegetarian routine. Products such as the bean series (soybeans and Lima beans are very rich in protein), eggs, "nutmeat" products, as well as gluten and soybean-based products are excellent. (There are commercial lines readily available almost worldwide today.)

Include plenty of leafy greens and at least one yellow vegetable every day. Eat fruit, preferably fresh whenever you get the chance, and two pieces (at least) a day if this is economically possible.

Lots of fluid intake is important. What's better than simple water? Nothing, in my set of books. Often it's best chilled (especially in hot weather). Give carbonated drinks and sugar-filled beverages the go-by. Pure fruit juices are excellent also. Besides being refreshing, they contain many important vitamins.

This will help maintain bowel regularity as well as enriching the system generally and raising the body resistance and the level of the pain threshold.

Another simple measure is to eat three or four prunes each night at bedtime. (Figs, dates, and raisins are good also. So are dried apricots.) This helps maintain excellent bowel activity.

Endeavor to get eight hours' sleep a night, every night. I don't care who you are or what you do, this is vital to good health. It will also help overcome your monthly problems like magic.

Exercise is essential. With your busy program you'll probably say flatly that you cannot afford the time. My rejoinder is, "What's so bad about a little time loss for exercise compared with time loss from pain and sheer exhaustion and inner frustration?"

If you don't feel inclined to race around the block, the simple exercises that are done in your own room are quite adequate. But these really do not compare with the simple systems such as running, jogging, or even going for a long walk.

When you exercise outdoors, inhale deeply, exhale fully. This all helps. Keep active. Don't lie about and feel sorry for yourself.

Now, what about drugs?

It is my belief that we're fast becoming a world of drug addicts. Everyone is seeking a cure in a pill bottle for every known ailment. However, if the suggestions above do not do the trick (and in the majority of cases they will after a few months of regular trying), resorting *on a temporary basis* to simple analgesics is reasonable.

Aspirin (in any of its multiple commercial packs) is usually quite sufficient. Take the minimum that will give relief. Repeat only if and when you must. Such pills are tolerated best after eating a meal, for they can sometimes initiate nausea or even vomiting if taken on an empty stomach.

It is absolutely imperative that you do not resort to strong drugs. (It is possible there may be some in the kitchen medicine cabinet. But do **NOT** get into the drug routine.)

Securing relief by using any alcohol-based product, of course, is sheer madness. It may give temporary relief, but it can establish habits which are more disastrous than dysmenorrhea will ever be. Similarly, don't try to secure relief from cigarettes. These, too, are nothing short of coffin nails. Medical science proves this.

I understand that certain hormones are now widely used for dysmenorrhea.

For persisting instances, a combination pill which consists of the hormones estrogen and progesterone (in low doses) may give excellent relief. This is sometimes given regularly (say from the fifth to the twenty-sixth days of the cycle, one daily). It can markedly reduce the severity of menstrual problems. However, in younger women, I do not like giving it for more than two to four months. It is amazing the way this, in association with the other recommendations, can completely eradicate the monthly problem in a relatively short time.

Let's be frank. Isn't this the same as The Pill?

Well, look at it this way. The Pill is a similar chemical formulation to this. Ideally, special packs endorsed for "gynecological reasons" are best prescribed for such problems. I am not keen on universally handing out The Pill to unmarried women, and conversely, many younger women are not keen to go on The Pill, even though it's for reasons apart from contraception.

I must ask this question at this point. Is it OK for women to go swimming or take baths and showers during menstruation, especially if they are dysmenorrhea victims?

Old ideas die hard. Of course it's perfectly safe. In fact, any person not having a daily shower in a country with a warm climate is sadly lacking in personal hygiene.

No harm can befall a girl just because she has a bath or a shower. Perhaps showers are best during the early active days of menstruation. Later, baths or showers are both quite suitable.

As far as swimming and surfing are concerned, in the first two or three days when menstrual flow may be reasonably heavy, local "problems" perhaps make it unwise. However, in the latter days when the flow is diminished, and with the current widespread use of internal tampons (with all their gimmicks and "protection devices") it doesn't really matter. The "social problem" is easily overcome. However, as far as its being injurious to health, this of course, is quite unfounded.

You mentioned earlier about irritability, mental depressions, and breast enlargement and tenderness. Is this the same as dysmenorrhea, or something separate?

It is certainly tied up with the system's hormonal output. But the exact modus operandi is perhaps a little different. We now know that in the days immediately preceding menstruation, there is a buildup of fluid in the system. This initiates a reaction in the brain. The kickbacks are psychological-type symptoms.

Happy people may suddenly become unhappy. A sour, unexplained disposition may suddenly overcome a girl who usually radiates sunshine and roses.

Often a series of unhappy, morose, depressed days follow in quick succession. Everything goes wrong. Nothing is right. The world is a gloomy, sad, unhappy place, fit for neither man nor beast. The extent of this might be transient. Or it may be deep-seated and severe. Sometimes the breast symptoms may accompany the syndrome. Or they may be the only symptom in sight.

Is there some simple cure for this?

As outlined earlier, the same set of "cures" will often assist in these cases also, but a favorable reaction is not always so easy to obtain.

We now find that many of these folk respond magically to the "oral diuretic" drugs. These effective and harmless tablets, taken as prescribed, will greatly increase the urinary flow for several days. Usually one tablet a day is needed. Commenced six to ten days before the expected onset of menstruation, the effect can be startling. The tense, painful breasts may vanish. The tender nipples become rapidly normal once more. The tense morose outlook is replaced by a smiling face.

Sometimes the diuretics alone are not quite enough. These cases may also need the added effect of a low-dose hormonal compound.

Can these pills be bought over the counter and taken as you have outlined?

My recommendation is that they be prescribed by a doctor and taken exactly as he recommends. In many countries they are regulated by governmental control, and may be purchased only under direct medical supervision. But I have given the information to let you know what is currently available and its true efficacy.

What is the normal amount of blood loss in menstruation?

This varies considerably. It ranges from 10 to 210 mls (2 teaspoonfuls to $^3/_4$ cup). The average is 40 mls (about 2.5 tablespoonfuls) per menstrual period.

A few queries from my mailbag would possibly be of interest right here. One young woman wrote:

"I often get a pain in the pelvic region half-way through the cycle. I've been told this could be appendicitis, but it seems strange it occurs every month."

This young lady is lucky. It's one of the sure signs that ovulation (release of the egg from the ovary) is taking place.

A little later on when she's married, it could be a valuable aid to her family-planning schedule. (More about this later.)

Another from the mailbag: "My periods are often early—like every twenty-one days. I often get tired and dizzy. Is this serious?"

This young lady is certainly losing more blood than she is capable of regenerating each month. Therefore the quality of her blood is suffering. Most likely she is suffering from a mild anemia. Plenty of iron-rich food (vegetables, fruit, etc.) is essential. If it continues, she definitely should seek medical advice in the hope of having this rectified.

Another wrote: "I am a young married mother twenty-one years old. Is it possible to become pregnant during menstruation?"

Personally I can never understand women who would desire to indulge in intercourse while menstruating. Nor a husband who could stand it either!

The chances of pregnancy are very small. Indeed, the "rhythm method" of birth control relies on the fact that ovulation takes place midcycle (when pregnancy is most probable). With no egg in the tube pregnancy is not possible. However, for unknown reasons, pregnancy has taken place on days very close to menstruation. It is not an infallible guide.

5

All About Boys

This sounds like an enchanting chapter heading. I'm sure the female section of your readers will probably start reading at this chapter!

Why not? After all, the relative "unknown" element in life is the one that arouses the most intrigue.

Still, in this modern age, I suppose everyone–but everyone–knows a fair amount about the opposite sex.

There is no doubt about that. A friend of mine who is a school teacher believes that by the time they leave primary school, 95 percent of his pupils know about 90 percent of the internal workings of the opposite sex.

That seems a wild statement. Do you believe it is true?

No, I don't. I believe he means that youngsters from the age of ten to twelve years onwards have a broad idea of generalities.

They are well aware that babies don't arrive by the stork. Neither do they grow under cabbages in the back garden. They also know that the doctor doesn't bring them in his black bag.

Especially if there are several children in the home, the

older children have usually followed events through pretty closely with their mother's altering shape over the months preceding another confinement.

Even toddlers know there's "another baby on the way, and Mommy is carrying him around inside her until the door opens."

Also, most are aware that "God planted a little seed inside Mommy, and it's been growing there for the past several months."

Do you think children instinctively know these facts, or do they have to be told?

The youthful, growing mind is like a sponge. In the early years it absorbs a staggering amount of information. A good deal of this is not of much immediate practical value. So it is stored away in the subconscious part of the brain. It lies there, ready and waiting for future use. Over the early formative years, odd pieces of detail are added, bit by bit. They, too, are stored away in the subsconscious filing system. Little ones will observe, listen, and quietly take facts in. They'll ask questions. The replies they receive are likewise stored away deep inside their subconscious. Later on they will read and hear other answers to their questions. The total amount is fed into their memory banks.

What is your opinion about parents answering their children's questions about sex?

There is no doubt about my feelings. It is of the greatest importance that parents give the child a factual reply. It must be prompt, accurate, to the point. Preferably it should be given in simple, understandable terms without embarrassment. If this is done right from the time the child can comprehend, an excellent rapport develops between parent and child.

Child asks question. Parent gives prompt, satisfying, accurate reply. Information is nonchalantly phased into the child's memory bank. As time progresses, he gradually starts to understand instinctively what we call "the facts of life."

The "Rooster Story"

Tell me your "rooster story" again. It always fascinates me!

Several times a year I go off to a small farm I have in the mountains. Or rather we all go—the whole family, which includes my wife and our four growing children.

There's nothing like a traditional farmyard to teach your family the general principles of life as it really is. The bits and pieces of general information you have given them start to mean something when they mix with the animals and the farm stock.

I'll never forget this particular day. Our youngest fellow was six years of age. Although he'd been given reasonable replies to the queries he'd raised from time to time, no formal sex instruction had ever been undertaken. One of his friends from the city had come to spend a few days with us during the school vacation. Not far away the hens were scratching around and pecking in the grass. With them was Joe, a virile young cockerel.

Suddenly Joe decided it was time to perform his fatherly act, and the usual skirmish with one of the hens took place.

The city lad was goggle-eyed. "Look, the rooster's killing the hen!" he cried out, and grabbed a stone to heave at the unlucky Joe.

However, my small son came to the rescue of Joe. "Don't be stupid," he said with obvious disgust. "He's only making her pregnant so her eggs will hatch out chickens!"

He thereupon gave the city slicker a short dissertation on the general topic of boy-girl relations in the farmyard.

There is little doubt his own observations on the property, together with bits of information he had heard, plus answers to questions he'd raised himself, had collectively welded together in his mind. In a sense, he was well versed in the basic matters of sex.

Then, in a way, your school teacher friend is about right when he talks about children having a wide range of general knowledge early in life?

In a sense, yes.

The Male Organs

Let's go into the story about boys in a bit more detail. We've outlined the internal workings of the female system pretty closely. Let's consider the male segment of the species in some detail.

Good idea. The obvious external characteristics of a male are the scrotum and the penis.

The penis is a soft elongated organ attached to the body where the legs meet. Its position approximates the vagina in the female. Under normal circumstances it hangs loosely. However, it is a remarkable organ, for its size and shape vary enormously under differing emotional circumstances.

The head is called the glans penis. This area is very sensitive. It is filled with millions of tiny nerve endings which react dramatically to certain forms of stimulation. The remainder of the length is occupied with a spongy material call the corpus cavernosum.

When the head is stimulated, or indeed even with certain mental thoughts, blood reflexly pours into the spongy tissue. Very rapidly the penis increases in size. It becomes taut and stiff, and an erection is said to have occurred.

Isn't the direction of the erect penis related to the female system?

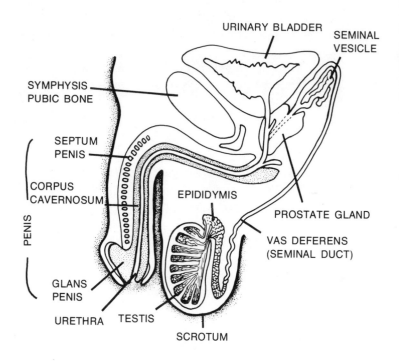

MALE ORGANS OF REPRODUCTION

This is a diagrammatic section of the external and internal reproductive male organs.

The penis normally hangs loosely downward. It is traversed by the narrow canal called the urethra. This transmits urine from the bladder to the exterior. But it also transports male cells (sperms) during intercourse.

It is formed of an inner spongy material that becomes engorged with blood during sexual stimulation (corpus cavernosum).

The loose baglike structure below and behind is called the scrotum. It houses the testes where the male cells are formed. The sperms travel via the epididymis, and later the vas deferens, up into the body to be stored in the seminal vesicles until they are discharged at intercourse.

Upon discharge they travel via the urethra to the exterior.

Yes. Instead of hanging in a downward direction, the erect organ stands upward and points forward. In fact, it exactly simulates the general size and shape and direction of the female vagina. This, of course, is intended to be. It facilitates the process of intercourse and makes the entire act an obvious and natural one.

Intercourse and reproduction are nature's own design. They are meant to be, and the entire male-female systems are basically geared for it.

I am quite certain that if any abnormal amount of effort was required for the process of reproduction, the worldwide birthrate would fall, man's liking for hard work being what it is.

Anthropologists will no doubt refute this. But nature has been kind, considerate, thoughtful. Everything is made extremely easy. Minimum work, minimum effort are required. This way nature cannot fail to succeed.

Don't you think this anatomical feature can breed problems for growing youth?

Very definitely.

Unfortunately, this is what many growing couples fail to remember. Virtually from the age of puberty on, the body is geared for reproduction. Nature has provided the basic essentials for this, and indeed there is nothing physically to stop it.

However, in our Christian society we believe it's in the best interest of everyone (the possible future baby included) for men and women to wait until marriage before they indulge in sexual intercourse.

The family unit is the best place to bring a baby home to. This is the best guarantee that he'll be safely reared and finally develop into a responsible citizen himself in due course.

Those who adhere to general Christian beliefs know that intercourse outside of marriage is not approved by God.

Quite apart from that, the laws of many lands do not permit unbridled sexual intercourse until a certain age has been attained by one or both parties. Indeed, statutory rape (as it is technically called) is a serious offense. This is intercourse with a girl under a certain legal age and is punishable at law even if the girl is a willing partner.

Jack and Jill

I'll never forget a complicated situation that occurred with two of my young patients not long ago.

Jack was twenty-one, had a good job, was earning a reasonable income, and had bright prospects for the future. Jill was his girl friend. She was aged sixteen the day they both came to see me.

However, she was well developed and certainly looked more than her youthful years. The pair had been friends for three years.

At this moment Jill happened to be pregnant. They were pretty sure of the situation and came along for my confirmation. My examination confirmed their strong suspicions.

"That's fine," said Jack. "We've planned to marry in any case. This will just hurry things up a bit." He wasn't very much concerned. Indeed, I think he was happy about the future prospects.

Marrying at sixteen is not my idea of the ideal in any circumstance. But Jill seemed satisfied with the idea too.

The next important move, of course, was to break the news to the respective parents. However, at that point the situation took on· a rather nasty twist.

Jack's parents were agreeable. "He's old enough to support a wife and family. He has a good job and an assured future. It's a sensible idea under the circumstances. Bad luck that they were indiscreet, but good luck to them for the future," was their general attitude.

But not so with Jill's mother and father. To put it in the vernacular, they "blew their stacks." "I'm gunning for him, Doc," the irate father bellowed when he visited me in my office to get proof of the story he'd been told.

It sounded a little theatrical. But what with his being an interstate truck driver, and a six-foot giant at that, I quavered a little as I thought of the unlucky Jack when the two should finally meet!

Jill's parents refused to sign the necessary legal documents, so there was only one alternative. The pair visited the local magistrate and presented the facts of the case.

Jill was pregnant. Jack had a good job and could support her. Jill's parents obstinately resisted a marriage. Could the magistrate intervene?

Being a kindly man, and well accustomed to the frailties of the human flesh, he agreed to override the parents' opinion and to let the pair legalize their misdemeanor.

But that was not the end of the story. In checking Jill's age, it immediately became obvious that she had conceived under the legal age which the law permits!

Therefore the police had to be summoned.

Problems started to mount for Jack. He now faced a police charge, that of statutory rape, even though the girl's consent was obvious at the time.

What now? Back to their friend the magistrate who'd been legally forced to reveal their secret.

He interposed on their behalf with the law. Jack was given a sentence, but this was reduced in view of the impending marriage. But he did have to pay a fine, even though it was greatly reduced in his particular case.

Many weeks of mental torture followed for Jill and Jack. Parental dissent, legal problems, difficulties with the law, an actual sentence!

The pair have since married. The baby has arrived. There are still major problems. The parents of Jill are unhappy and refuse to see her or the baby. It has brought a permanent family rift with her home and some of her friends and relatives. What the future holds in store is anybody's guess. In my opinion, it is shaky, and runs a high risk of foundering. I hope the basic morals of this true story are obvious. They are being repeated every day sometime, someplace.

I merely tell it to emphasize the fact that although our bodies are built and geared for sexual intercourse from an early age, don't be fooled into the temptation.

Sure it's easy! But the problems it can generate before we're socially prepared can be dramatic. Never forget that!

I'd guess that Jack and Jill won't forget the facts for the rest of their lives.

How true!

More Facts About the Male

Could we proceed a bit further with our rundown on boys?

Fine! We've discussed the first organ, the penis, in a little detail. It is traversed by a fine tube called the uretha. This tube has a twofold function. It is part of the urinary tract. In this way it transports the waste fluid of the body (urine) from the bladder, where it is temporarily stored, to the outside.

Second, it carries material called seminal fluid to the exterior also. This is the fluid that contains the male reproductive cells that are called sperms.

The sperms are discharged only during sexual intercourse (or when the male is sexually stimulated). By a simple system of valves, the bladder is closed off at this time so that there is

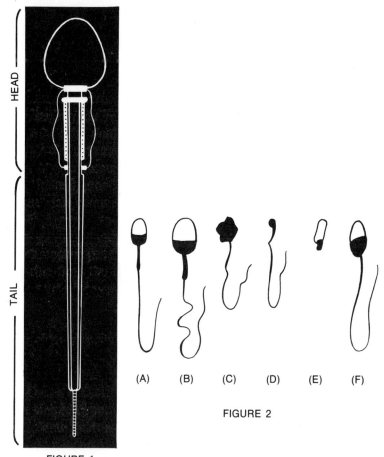

FIGURE 1

FIGURE 2

THE MALE REPRODUCTIVE CELL

This is the "spermatozoon" (or "sperm" for short), the male cell of reproduction.

Produced continuously by the testes, enormous numbers are manufactured. Indeed, in one single emission up to 700 million male cells are released (and it takes only **one** to produce a pregnancy!).

Figure 1 shows the normal shape of the male sperm. It has a head and a tail portion. It is essential that the tail move freely to help propel it along.

In Figure 2, diagram (a) is the normal sperm. Diagrams (b) to (f) are "abnormal" sperms. These are not likely to reproduce. If a large number of these are normally present in the seminal fluid, problems and difficulties in becoming pregnant may occur.

automatically no chance that the two fluids will be mixed up.

Where are the male cells formed?

The sperms are manufactured in the scrotum. This is the loose, saclike structure situated behind and below the penis.

Located inside the scrotum are two roundish, firm organs named the testes. They are the male counterpart of the female ovary. Their job is to produce a nonstop supply of male cells—the spermatozoa, or simply sperms for short.

Actually, the production of sperms starts at the age of puberty, when other characteristic secondary sex features start to develop. It then proceeds for fifty years or more.

In certain animals the manufacture of sperms occurs only at certain times of the year. But with the human race it is a continuing process. Indeed, medical records bulge with amazing feats of reproduction in males of astounding ages.

From the testes the sperms are transported along a narrow canal that conveys them toward the body. This is called the epididymis where it commences in the scrotum.

As it proceeds upward into the body, it is called the vas deferens.

Inside the body the sperms then enter a reservoir called the seminal vesicle. Here the male cells are stored until they are needed.

From the seminal vesicle a small tube joins into the urethra.

It is important that the male sperms have plenty of fluid in which to move around. Otherwise they would soon die. The fluid from the prostate also gives them food and keeps them active and well nourished.

Under the Microscope

What does a sperm actually look like?

Under the high-powered microscope, it looks like a tadpole! (Doesn't sound very attractive, does it?)

It has a largish, pointed head. After this, there is a long tail. Fresh sperms are very active. Their tails waggle at a high speed, and this is the way they move along. Indeed, they can race along at the rate of one to three centimeters a minute. For such minute organisms this is fast moving.

Don't the testes produce hormones as well as sperms?

Yes. Just as the ovary produces important chemicals called hormones, so the testes produce male hormones. The hormone is called testosterone. This important chemical gives males their characteristic appearance.

These hormones accelerate production at the age of puberty. They are poured directly into the bloodstream and are carried to all parts of the system. They exert a profound influence on the body. The well-known characteristics of growing youth quickly set in. Hair commences to grow on the face, under the arms, in the pubic area near the sex gland, and often on the chest as well.

The larynx or voice box develops, and the voice "breaks." That means it becomes deeper in tone and characteristically "male."

Muscles develop, and the typical masculine male development takes place. The sex organs develop, the penis becomes longer and larger, and the testes start producing the male cells. All other tubes and glands of sex ducts increase in size and activity as well.

Tremendous psychological changes also occur. The boy becomes more mature in his outlook. There is an attraction for the opposite sex. His desire for female companionship starts nibbling at him. With increasing years, a "desire" for sex gradually builds up. Indeed, erotic thoughts (as they are called) often fill his mind. As the sperm reservoirs fill with male cells, often to the point of overflowing, he frequently has dreams at night, and this results in seminal emissions. Unbeknown to him (because he is asleep) the reservoirs suddenly contract, and a mass of cells and fluid pours forth into the urethra and flows from the point of the penis. These are commonly referred to as "wet dreams."

Don't some boys get a guilt complex about this?

Yes, many do. They have some hidden belief that this is wrong or evil. But it is quite normal. It is essential for the reservoir to empty every so often to make room for the oncoming cell production. There is nothing evil, sinful, or diabolical about nocturnal emissions. No guilt is attributed to the boy. In fact, it is an indication that he is normal and healthy and that his systems are operating as they are supposed to. He should welcome the emissions and not be perplexed about them.

Millions—but a Short Life

How many male cells are there in a single emission?

This varies a good deal. With each emission, whether it be a normal nocturnal one or an emission occurring with actual intercourse, between two and four mls. of fluid are involved. In this there are up to 700 million male cells! It's an enormous number, isn't it! It's like the huge number of potential eggs that are housed in the ovary in the female. On the average 200 million are present. It varies with each individual. But one vital aspect is certain: There is a superabundance there.

I've been cautioning youngsters who like to play with fire —or indulge in premarital sex (to be more precise)—that each time they engage in intercourse, between 200 and 700 million male cells are injected into the female system. And each cell is capable of initiating a pregnancy!

It staggers the imagination, doesn't it? The possibilities are terrifying.

But don't the male cells soon die off?

Yes, their life-span is not long. Nobody is sure exactly how long they live. Most of the physiology experts say: "The survival time of sperms introduced into the vagina has not been determined with accuracy. It may be a day or two."

In a preceding chapter you said that pregnancy can take place only when a sperm contacts the female egg when it is in the fallopian tube, and this is about two to three days in any given menstrual month. Doesn't this then limit the possibility of pregnancy enormously?

Yes, it certainly does. In *theory* there are only three to four days each month when pregnancy is possible. However, from the practical point of view, things are a bit different. Nature has a lot of funny little quirks. What's *supposed* to happen often doesn't, and vice versa.

Besides, nature usually doesn't give "Stop" and "Go" signs like street lights. Things just quietly smolder on inside the system. In the main, we are oblivious to what is taking place within our bodies. No sudden sign jumps out and says, "Ovulation Today—Be Careful."

In fact, the reverse takes place. The hormonal makeup of the system usually pressurizes our emotions. This is all aimed at helping nature with the inherent intent of reproducing.

Many couples become most amorous at the time each month when a pregnancy is most likely to result from foolish indiscretions. You see, nature in itself doesn't have any moral scruples. Although it is aimed at reproducing and does everything to this end, it leaves the final decision to you.

You and your personal moral code, in the ultimate, make the step.

Happiness Is Petting --
Unhappiness Is Carrying
a Baby! (Sometimes)

We've talked a little about "sex" and "attraction" and "hormones" and all that. Why not get down to the details of lovemaking?

That's a good idea. I'm sure everybody is just waiting for us to get around to this very important topic. After all, it's supposed to be the basic ingredient in life.

Do you equate "love" with "sex"?

Not really, but I know that lots of people (and heaps of teen-agers) do. Our crazy society is trying to make us believe the two are synonymous. If you watch TV and read the papers for a few days, you get the general impression that romance, infatuation, falling in love, racing around half naked, indulging in sexual intercourse (but seldom, if ever, becoming pregnant) are virtually one and the same thing.

This is generally done up in a wrapper which informs us that to be attractive to the opposite sex all these attributes are vital. It's pushed a bit further too. Usually a product creeps into the picture. Therefore, the story enlarges out to this: Wear "Brand X" of this product (eg, perfume, hair spray, lipstick, cosmetic, underwear, nightie), and you'll be an

instant-success sex kitten. You will immediately conquer the
heart of the man of your desire. He will literally fall head over
heels in love with you.

"In love"—whatever that means.

In the eyes of the advertising men, it really means this:
Wear this erotic perfume (nightie, underwear, hair spray,
cosmetic, brassiere, girdle, bikini, or whatnot), and your
feminine anatomical details will be accentuated to anyone
who has two eyes in his head. This in turn will arouse his
hormones, and he will become sexually attracted to you.

In other words, you'll be playing to the sensual gratifications of the male to whom your charms are directed.

*So as far as the male is concerned, many of the outer signs
of female adornment are purely traps to arouse his emotional
sensations?*

Absolutely yes. Commerce has long since recognized the
power of sex in selling. It realizes that women love to be
"wanted." Anything that will offer them this prospect, in
their belief, is "good advertising." Merely because it will
make them purchase the commodity under question.

About the only other ingredient in life that many people are
interested in, apart from desire and sex and all that, is money.
Join the two, and you have the god of the multitudes. And you
have the god of big business.

What is Love?

*What, then, is your idea of love? Surely there must be some
relationship between love and sex.*

Very definitely.

There are all sorts of love. The Scriptures say, "God is
love." But this has nothing to do with sensuous gratification,
even though God created man and woman and their sensory
systems. He told them to multiply and replenish the earth,

and in a sense He is responsible for the way they feel at all times. He also made their hormonal systems, and their nervous systems, and gave them the ability to appreciate one another in every sense of the word.

God's love for mankind is that of an ever-present Father. His delight, according to the Scriptures, is to see people walk in the paths of righteousness. In other words, God likes His children to be upstanding, forceful, intelligent men and women, acting as law-abiding, honest citizens.

This is one sort of love.

What are some of the other types?

There is the love that exists between a mother and her infant. Call this maternal love if you like. It is something that has no counterpart in any other relationship. It is a warm, deep affection. It has a deep attachment, for the infant is literally part of the mother, and she treats it as such.

Then there is the continued love of parents for their growing children. The intimate relationship of family life breeds this special type of emotional bond. This is usually appreciated more by the parent than by the offspring. But with the passage of time, today's child is tomorrow's parent. Then the cycle starts all over again.

I often recall my parents saying to me when I was young: "You do not understand how a parent feels about his children—how we feel about you. But one day, when you are a parent, you'll understand."

Now that time has come; I understand. So will any parent reading this book.

Let's talk about love as it applies to other things.

Sure. We're always hearing people say, "I love this," and "I simply love that!" In essence, all they are saying is that they have some vague sort of desire for a certain item. It may be a garment, a special food, a particular sweet, a type of vacation, or a new and swanky sports car.

"Love" is confused with "like" or "appreciate." There is no real, deep, sincere bond between the person and the item they're speaking of. These words are often thrown about with gay abandon. They are virtually meaningless, so far as sincerity is concerned.

What about sex and love, then?

When two people, a boy and a girl, say they love each other, it may be in one of two categories.

The commonest inference is that they are emotionally attracted to one another. We know that opposites attract. This is basic physics. Boy and girl are no different, and they stick to the law with relentless fervor! The basic hormonal makeup of the two sexes is that there is a violent attraction between the two. But down deep, it is purely a chemical reaction. I hate saying this, but it is the fact of the situation.

You mean falling in love is merely a test-tube chemical reaction?

It sounds terribly callous when analyzed and recorded in cold print, but that is essentially the gist of the situation.

As we discussed earlier, the basic intention of nature is to keep the race going. It wants, beyond everything else, to encourage reproduction. New lives (and as many as possible) is its aim. The entire boy-girl system is geared to this end. We've been endowed with a brisk hormonal system that strives hard to this end point.

Boys produce male chemicals. These pervade every cell in their systems and give them a basic desire for the opposite sex. Conversely, female chemicals are produced in the female. They are carried by the bloodstream throughout the system. They create an urge for male companionship and nearness.

Now, as it so happens, lots of people believe that this basic attraction is "love." But it is nothing more than a natural attribute that covers every sphere of the animal kingdom.

Take a look around. The animals reproduce, yet you could hardly say they were "in love." Similarly, trees and flowers (most of which have a definite sex cycle in their reproduction) aren't "in love," whatever your definition of the word might possibly be.

True Love

This all sounds a bit disquieting. Are you really trying to knock "love" for a loop?

Not really. I'm merely trying to point out the difference between true love and imagined love. There is a basic difference, and this is most important.

In other words, we could say that sexual attraction and basic, mature, emotional love are two separate items and worlds apart in their true meaning.

This is the second category of love I planned to mention.

Whereas sexual attraction receives full satisfaction in "making love" or merely "having sex," mature emotional love is far more. It comes usually with marriage, or rather with several years of married life.

Certainly sex plays an important part. But added to the sex element is a sincere, deep attachment of two lives that have been united and woven into a pattern of oneness. There is a unity of purpose, a similar pattern of thought, an understanding that exists between those two people alone.

There is a warm affection that goes far beyond the immediate sexual gratification of the moment. There is an appreciation for each other's needs, for the desires of each partner, for their respective likes and dislikes. One will go out of his way to assist the other. Efforts at making each other happy and content are made. This yields a serenity and a warm secure feeling that only a successful blending of two lives can possibly yield.

Don't you think this all sounds a little ethereal? Do you believe it assists for real in this mad hustling world of dog-eat-dog?

I certainly do. You've only to look around you to see it working on all sides.

Maybe it's not so obvious on the surface. I think the people who are most in love prefer to keep the good news to themselves. But it reflects in a happy personality, a bright disposition, a contented manner.

Now that you've pointed out the two basic types of "love," what is the practical application of this?

I was hoping you'd ask me that, for it is very important.

I think growing teen-agers must be aware that their ultimate future happiness is not wrapped up in the immediate sensual gratifications of the moment. Sex exists, for sure. And it is perhaps at its height in terms of desiring to be expressed in the early years of life. But remember this is merely one aspect. Sex wasn't invented to be flaunted and to be shared with every willing partner around town. Lots of growing girls believe it is (much to their sorrow as the years advance).

Rather than "carry on" whenever the opportunity offers and with whomever is available, it is far more sensible (in terms of lifelong happiness and inner peace of mind) to be careful, especially in the premarital years.

When you find your partner and settle down to married life and the establishment of a home for keeps, there'll be plenty of time to do all the things you wanted to do (including the things your friends said you were a fool not to experiment with beforehand).

Premarital Sex

Let's be frank. I take it you're knocking premarital sex?

As a practicing physician I do not condone it. Personally, I have a moral code that tells me it's "not right."

But apart from that, my experience has shown me on hundreds of occasions that it is unwise as well. Indeed, it has often produced alarming and disastrous results, affecting more than one person.

I doubt that a week passes but some forlorn young lady comes into my office with "her problem."

In fact, I believe I can almost read her mind before she starts talking.

What happens?

In general terms, it usually goes like this: Enter Miss X. (One single glance and two seconds is all it requires to size things up.) Sits down. Eyes look floorward. Lips tremble. Silence.

So, to prod her along a little, I open up:

"Good morning. How are you today?" (or "What's your name?" or "Nice day, isn't it?" Anything to break the silence.)

She: "Good morning." (More silence.)

Me: "Well, now, what's your problem?" (A good opener. Doesn't offend, and she must have a problem or she wouldn't be here. The problem is pretty obvious by now, for she looks fit otherwise.)

She: "Well—er—I have a problem."

(That's it. Right again. She's staring at the ceiling at this stage, trying to look unruffled, but I know her heart is beating 150 to the minute, and her nerves are clawing her almost to death. She hates every moment of it. It's not so bad if she's been a regular patient for years. But mostly I haven't seen her before. She's too scared to go to the family doctor for fear he'll tell her parents, and then there would be the devil to pay.)

Me: "A problem? [Surprise!] Well, plenty of people have problems. Don't be too upset. Most problems can be solved." (That's true, but solving them is often another problem in itself.)

She: "It's like this. I seem to have missed my last monthly."

Me: "Oh, well, this happens to lots of people. Often there is some basic cause for it. I know a young lady that misses her periods whenever she changes jobs, which is every year or two."

She: "Really! But I think mine is a bit different."

Me: "Well, plenty of women become pregnant, you know. It's part of life."

At this point she often starts weeping copiously. Or she may take the hard line and start on about her boyfriend and what a beast he's been or else how foolish she was, or she simply "didn't understand," or she'd planned to take The Pill but somehow hadn't got around to it.

The possibilities are endless.

But invariably one cold fact comes through. The girl is pregnant! What now?

That IS a good question. What now?

One thing is certain. Irrespective of how sad she is at the moment, I can give her a written guarantee that in "x" months' time (maybe seven or eight) she'll give birth to a real, live baby! Now, to a teen-ager who isn't married, this is a very sobering thought.

Especially if she's been brought up in a conservative home where "Sex-out-of-marriage Is Sin" (there are still lots of homes around like this), the problem factor mounts progressively.

The Answer to the Problem

What's the answer to the problem?

The key to the problem at this moment is not to sermonize, irrespective of my own personal beliefs on the subject. Invariably I endeavor to give the girl what assistance is possible. Trying to placate her is frequently the most difficult immediate task.

Then follows an explanation of the possible lines of action. In many countries legalized abortion is now available, and thousands of young women afflicted with this personal problem rush off and take this line of action.

However, in my town it is not legal; nor is it particularly desirable—in my town or any other. Therefore, my patient has to face the fact of an impending confinement.

The next item is to get the message across to her parents. This is very often a task of major magnitude.

How do parents take the tidings?

It varies enormously. Some take it without batting an eye. Others become enraged and virtually throw their daughters out on the streets. Believe it or not, but this is quite common in supposedly updated, sophisticated, Christian countries. Sheer bigotry, together with a sense of shame, causes some parents to do things they would not dream of doing if they were thinking clearly.

I'll never forget an incident that took place when I was practicing years back in a small country town.

One of the local girls became involved in the manner just described. Her age was a mere seventeen summers. She was too terrified to broach the news to her parents, particularly her father. To help her out, I offered to discuss the matter with him. What followed left me in a turmoil. The father almost took off into outer space. He was infuriated. He yelled about "family disgrace," the "uselessness of the rising generation," "dishonesty," and every other possible insinuation about the daughter's lack of principle.

The mother took the facts quietly and said she believed it was their duty to do all they could for their girl. This, of course, was the sensible approach.

The father continued to rage on unabated. Not only did he blame the girl, but he was literally going to get the "no-good boyfriend and tear him to shreds." In fact, before the night was out, he had called the local police to assist in his cause.

As far as the girl was concerned, he was "through with her." She would be tossed out of the family circle forthwith. He was finished with her, and that was final! The tirade went on into the wee small hours.

Finally the father and mother left, and I went to bed—exhausted.

The following day the local officer called at my office. In his arms he carried a big book. After the usual opening pleasantries, we got down to the facts of life, in this case, the young lady of the previous night.

"The old fellow seemed a trifle upset," the officer said.

"He certainly did," I replied. "He seems to be the moral guardian of the entire nation, let alone the local town."

"That's the impression he gave, isn't it!" he went on. "Here, take a look at this."

He placed the big book he was carrying on the table. It opened at a marked page.

The book happened to be the court record from the local courthouse. It was an old edition. But written in words bold and clear was the full name of our father friend from the night before. And written in indelible ink was a very unsavory charge made against him a few year before. He was charged (and convicted) of a grave sex offense against a local young lady. He had spent a considerable time in the local jail!

As it happened, he had later married the same girl. This, no doubt, had freed his conscience of his debt to society and to the young lady in particular. But instead of pursuing a happy, normal life, he had quietly nurtured an inner grudge. This came to bursting point when his own daughter in turn was involved in a set of circumstances rather similar to his own.

In the overwhelming majority of cases parents have been through the mill in one form or another before. Most are filled with concern and compassion for their child who has turned a foot on the wrong path and has been unfortunate enough to be ensnared.

Usually a conference is arranged, and we all have a down-to-earth discussion on the line of action that seems best to follow.

I prefer both parents to be there, mother and father, plus the girl, and, if possible, also the boy involved and his parents, too, if this is feasible. (Usually it is not. So often the fellow takes the easy way out and flies the coop.)

The simplest expedient, of course, is for the couple to marry. But the simple solution is often not the best one. A marriage built on an unwanted pregnancy is highly likely to falter at an early stage.

Sometimes the parents are willing to raise the child as their own. I take my hat off to them, But this, too, breeds problems.

Who is the true mother? Who gives the orders, and who does the infant look to as time passes by? Major problems usually arise, and these are often serious obstacles to domestic harmony.

Many others take another simple alternative and arrange for the baby to be adopted out at birth. This is usually carried out through the local governmental department. It is quick, quiet, effective, and solves the problem.

But it takes a long time to heal the scar on the young mother's mind and in her heart.

Happiness Is—

These are interesting stories. What do you have to say as a final summing up of "happiness" and "love"?

Whenever possible I try to get the message across to my youthful patients and friends that their inner chemical factories produce tremendously powerful products. In fact, they are often so powerful that under certain circumstances the factory products can simply take over. When this occurs, disaster stalks. Not only disaster, but unhappiness, problems, inner misgivings, mental turmoil, and even physical hardship, if you happen to weaken and give in.

Let's not be mid-Victorian about the subject. Sexual intercourse may be fun. But sexual intercourse is not love and when pursued for lustful reasons alone, does nothing for the system, for prolonged happiness, or for the personality.

Why not preserve your chastity for the time when you can develop your association into true, meaningful love? This comes with marriage and the choice of a suitable life partner. Then it can strengthen as the years pass by. Every year the bond and fellowship become firmer. Inner peace of mind develops and finally takes over.

In the long term, mental equanimity and peace of mind are the most important ingredients to happiness. This can be yours, for years and years.

I am not speaking as a theorist on this matter. I pass on the information from practical experience accumulated over many years and after dealing with many youngsters from all walks of life.

I hope you'll give the subject more than a passing thought.

7

Where DO Babies Come From?

You've been delivering babies for many years now. What's your opinion of the baby business?

I find it great. In fact, it's exhilarating. I never cease to marvel at the miraculous phenomenon. I'm afraid you never become entirely accustomed to the astounding fact that a brand-new life can be achieved with such ease.

A baby can be produced with comparatively little thought, and certainly not much real effort, on the part of the mother. (I'm talking in general terms and am certainly not depreciating the physical efforts involved at the time of delivery.)

Labor is hard work, believe me. (It's hardest of all for the mother, but it can have its problems for the nursing staff and the medical staff too.)

But compare the feat with the production of, say, an automobile or a piece of machinery, and I must agree with you—it is comparatively easy.

Getting anything into production is a major mechanical achievement. There are plans, and more plans, and conferences, and meetings, and sketches, and designs, and models, and so on and so on.

Then there is the modus operandi in transferring everything from the paper plans to reality. Then there are the problems of making sure nothing goes wrong on the production line.

I have several patients who are engaged in production of physical products. Each one's life is one eternal headache trying to cope with the never-ending multiplicity of problems.

But in the "manufacture" of a baby, there is none of that!

How right you are! For sure, we have our moments. Many things can go wrong. But for every one that causes problems, there must be eight or nine others that cause no trouble at all. Nature very kindly rolls merrily along. Bit by bit, in its own marvelous way, it takes charge of the entire production line. From beginning to end, nature takes over.

In earlier chapters we went over some of the basics of reproduction. We dealt with the female angle, then the male part. What say we now combine the two and find out exactly how reproduction takes place?

That's a good idea. I know most of our readers know much of the theory of reproduction quite well; however, some will not be familiar with the story, so we'll go right from the start.

The Cause of Pregnancy

What causes pregnancy in the first place?

Pregnancy takes place when a male cell (or spermatozoon) contacts and unites with a female cell (or ovum). When this occurs, fertilization of the ovum is said to have taken place.

The male cells are deposited inside the female during the act of intercourse. The penis actually penetrates the female genital tract (vagina), and during a pleasurable sensation, termed orgasm, about half a teaspoonful of male seminal fluid containing the sperms is released high up in the vagina.

Didn't you say earlier that the sperms literally wag their tails to propel themselves along?

Yes. Under the microscope they appear as elongated little fellows with vigorously wagging tails. They race along at the rate of one to three centimeters a minute. However, they have a long, long way to go before they reach their goal.

Although an average of 200 million sperms are released at intercourse, only one will ultimately give rise to a pregnancy if it happens to encounter a female ovum.

What a terrible death rate for the rest!

Yes, but they stoically put up with that. In fact, one supersperm often seems to be making better headway than his brothers. As he proceeds to his goal, his brethren simply lie down and die in his track. In so doing, they produce a chemical called hyaluronidase. This is a potent substance which eventually helps the sperm bore a hole in the ovum once he has found it. This is brotherly love to the ultimate degree, don't you think?

But surely it must take the male cell an awfully long time to swim this vast distance in an uncharted sea. How does he manage to do it without assistance?

This is a question to which there is no satisfactory known answer. Researchers know that the sperms lose their "motility" or tail-wagging, propelling power within sixty minutes outside a uterus.

However, once inside the uterus itself they'll keep this up for thirty or forty hours.

Besides this, it is believed the uterus itself plays a part in helping the sperms penetrate. After intercourse, the uterus apparently undergoes sustained contraction. Then it suddenly relaxes. At the same instant it sucks up the contents of the vagina (including most of the 200 million sperms), and within moments these become deeply placed in the uterus, and indeed may be thrust right into the Fallopian tubes themselves. It has been shown experimentally that this can occur within minutes or even seconds after intercourse.

Does the female ovum have any "come hither" attraction to the male cell?

According to my physiology experts, there is no evidence that the ovum exerts a positive chemical attraction. Therefore, you might say, the sperms reach their goal by sheer good luck rather than by following road signs or any other encouraging advice en route.

The Fertility of the Male

I've heard that some males have "sperm problems," and this can reduce their fertility rating. Is this so?

Very definitely. It's been found that if the total sperm count falls to 60 million or less, fertility is markedly reduced. In other words, the female is not so likely to become pregnant even under ideal conditions.

Often the sperms have deformed appearances. If more than 20 percent are so affected, fertility again drops sharply. Of course it is essential the sperms be actively motile. Their tails must be waving frantically all the time. Otherwise their process of locomotion fails. It isn't much use having a car whose wheels won't turn. It won't get you anywhere. Similarly with the sperms. Take away their movement function, and disaster lurks. Possible pregnancy chances receive a blow.

You will remember that a diagram in chapter 5 shows what sperms look like under the microscope.

How are all these millions of cells numbered and described?

It is really quite simple. The pathologists have special techniques. They obtain a specimen of seminal fluid from a patient (usually when the couple are having difficulty in reproducing). A "sperm count" is carried out. A certain number of the cells are actually counted in a special counting chamber under the microscope. This is then multiplied by a certain factor, and the actual number of sperms in each millilitre of fluid is calculated. At the same time, their motility is noted, and the "abnormal forms" worked out as well.

Often when we're investigating a married couple ex-

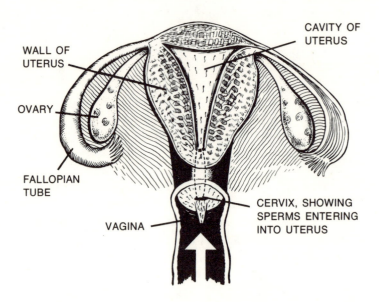

DIAGRAMMATIC PICTURES OF PREGNANCY:
(1) RELEASE OF MALE CELLS

The following series of diagrams shows the story of pregnancy from the moment sexual intercourse occurs until the baby is finally born.

The picture above shows the male cells (sperms) entering the female reproductive system via the cervical canal and uterus. They penetrate outward into the fallopian tubes where fertilization of the female cell, the ovum, occurs.

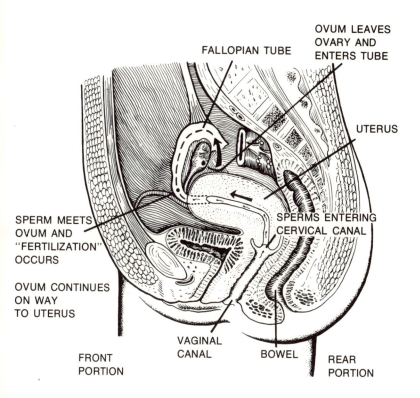

FALLOPIAN TUBE

OVUM LEAVES
OVARY AND
ENTERS TUBE

UTERUS

SPERM MEETS
OVUM AND
"FERTILIZATION"
OCCURS

SPERMS ENTERING
CERVICAL CANAL

OVUM CONTINUES
ON WAY
TO UTERUS

FRONT
PORTION

VAGINAL
CANAL

BOWEL

REAR
PORTION

(2) COURSE TAKEN BY MALE SPERMS AND FEMALE OVUM

The male cells (sperms) enter the womb (uterus) at the neck of the uterus (cervix). They actively swim into the womb, to the uppermost part, then outward into the fallopian tubes.

At ovulation (about the fourteenth day of the menstrual cycle) the female egg (ovum) is released from the ovary where it is manufactured. It enters the far end of the fallopian tube and is swept downward toward the cavity of the womb.

Meeting a male cell in the tube, union occurs. The two cells unite and become one. However, the united cell then actively divides, divides, divides, and redivides (it is now called a morula) as it pursues its course down toward the womb.

Reaching the womb, it rapidly becomes embedded in the lining, and pregnancy is well established.

A new life has started, and the minute baby (called a fetus) quickly begins to form.

periencing pregnancy difficulties ("infertility," as it's called), this is one of the earliest tests carried out. It is essential to establish whether it is the male or the female wherein the difficulty lies.

It is invariably one or the other. Unfortunately, when there is a marked depression of male cells, or other problems here, treatment becomes a major task.

What Happens in the Fallopian Tube

We last left the sperm in the fallopian tube. What is the next event in the pregnancy sequence?

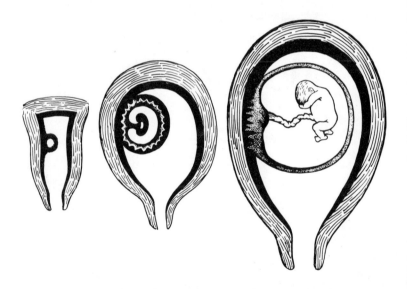

(3) APPEARANCE OF DEVELOPING BABY IN WOMB

The fertilized egg quickly becomes established in the lining of the womb, which has been prepared to receive it.

Shortly, a fluid-filled sac forms around the developing fetus, and the new life inside continues its course of increasing in size.

Next in line is the actual linking of the two cells. This occurs in the outer part of the tube. At this point, the female ovum is being vigorously swept toward the interior of the uterus by the lining cells which have minute hairlike brushes on top of them. These set up a wave current pushing in the direction of the uterus. In addition, the tube itself has contraction waves sweeping inward. The combined effect is to push the egg along. This it does at a fairly rapid rate, and the

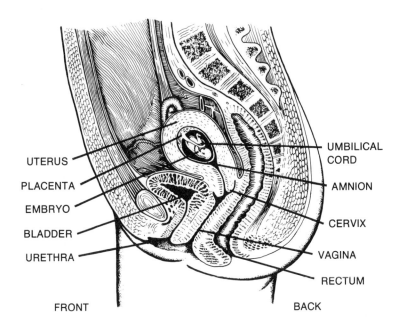

UTERUS

PLACENTA

EMBRYO

BLADDER

URETHRA

UMBILICAL CORD

AMNION

CERVIX

VAGINA

RECTUM

FRONT   BACK

(4) FETUS CONTINUES TO DEVELOP

The new life, called an embryo in the early stages, and a fetus later on, gradually develops. The accommodating uterus increases in size. The obvious outward sign, of course, is a gradual swelling in the lower part of the body. The swelling wells up from the pelvic areas into the abdominal region.

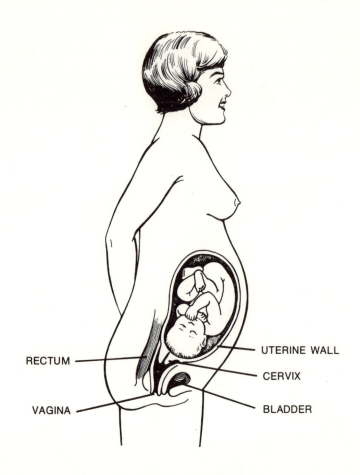

RECTUM

UTERINE WALL

CERVIX

VAGINA

BLADDER

(5) BIRTH IS IMMINENT

After nine months it's time for baby to be born. This picture shows the approximate position of baby just before the start of a normal labor.

Generally the head is in the lower position. The abdominal protrusion is usually quite marked; breast development and enlargement is generally well advanced also.

journey is usually completed within three to four days. However, once the sperm penetrates the ovum, the cells commence to multiply at a rapid rate.

Isn't this the instant when the hereditary factors are linked?

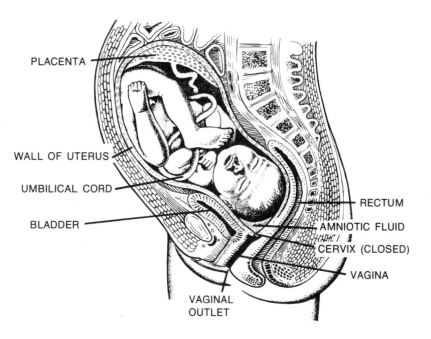

PLACENTA

WALL OF UTERUS

UMBILICAL CORD

BLADDER

RECTUM

AMNIOTIC FLUID

CERVIX (CLOSED)

VAGINA

VAGINAL OUTLET

(6) LABOR ABOUT TO COMMENCE

A close-up "sectional" view of baby just as labor is about to commence. The cervix is tightly closed at this stage. Note the umbilical cord connecting baby (at the point where his navel will later occur) with the placenta.

This is his lifeline, and it is essential it remain intact until he has been delivered. It transports vital oxygen and food to him up until the instant his oxygen supply commences via his own airways when he starts yelling shortly after birth.

Headfirst is the normal delivery. Sometimes, a "breech" (or bottom-first) delivery occurs, but this has more difficulties. Fortunately it only represents a small proportion of deliveries.

Yes. Male and female cells each contain minute structures called chromosomes. Scattered along the length of these are little knobs termed genes. This is the way hereditary characteristics are transmitted.

In normal body cells the chromosomes exist in pairs; but, as part of the process of producing an ovum (and also a

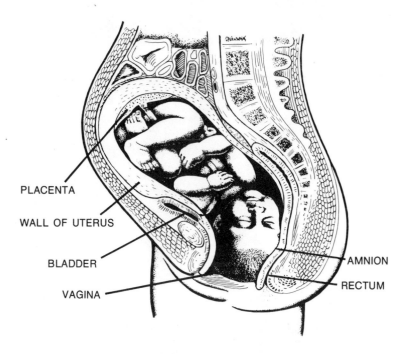

PLACENTA

WALL OF UTERUS

BLADDER

VAGINA

AMNION

RECTUM

(7) LABOR WELL ADVANCED

"Labor" is the word given to the process of birth of the baby. "Delivery" means baby has actually made his entry into the big wide world.

Here he is well on the way. The neck (or cervix) portion of the womb has fully opened up ("dilated"), and baby is gradually coming down through the cervical opening and vaginal canal. These parts distend in a remarkable manner during the stages of labor.

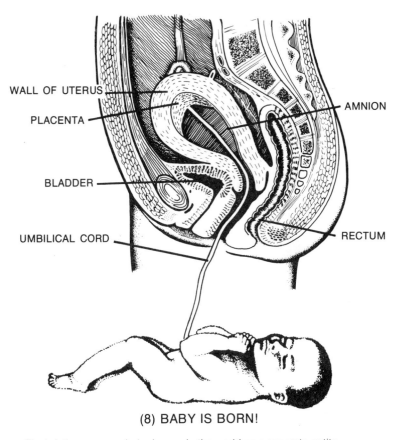

WALL OF UTERUS

PLACENTA

BLADDER

UMBILICAL CORD

AMNION

RECTUM

(8) BABY IS BORN!

Final delivery means baby is now in the world as a separate entity.

Here he is now, quite separate from his mother. He is still connected to the placenta via the vital umbilical cord. Blood still pulsates into his system.

In a moment or two he will give a lusty yell, taking aboard his own independent supply of fresh oxygen-containing air. At this juncture the cord becomes redundant.

Soon after, the placenta will peel off from the wall of the womb and be discharged via the vaginal canal as the "afterbirth" of the confinement. It, too, is of no further use.

Baby's cord is clamped (or tied) and cut. He is now an independent life.

However, he will be dependent upon the loving care and attention of his mother for several years yet to come! (As every mother knows so well.)

The creation of a new life is still the most wondrous event possible. It is the end point of God's great capacity for new life.

sperm), each pair is split so that the number of chromosomes each carries is halved. When the one male cell and the one female cell unite at fertilization, the number of chromosomes is again brought back to the normal number. But half are from the male cell, and the other half are from the female cell. Therefore, there is a blending of the characteristics of the two parents.

The next question is, what happens to the fertilized ovum?

Over the next few days, during which time it gradually moves down the fallopian tube, the united cell rapidly multiplies. The single cell divides into two. These two become four, then eight, sixteen, thirty-two, sixty-four, and so on. By the time it has reached the uterus, a mass of cells has developed. This is called a morula. Very quickly these cells arrange themselves into an outer layer and an inner mass.

As we mentioned before, the lining of the uterus (called the endometrium) gears itself each month to receive a fertilized ovum. If this does not occur, the entire lining is shed in the form of a normal menstrual bleed. This is the typical monthly routine of women who are not pregnant. However, once pregnancy takes place, an entirely different process occurs.

Somehow (and we still don't know how) the message that fertilization has taken place is transmitted back to the ovary (from whence the ovum came in the first place).

You might recall that the space the egg occupied before it was shed now forms into a body called the corpus luteum. This begins to produce potent hormones, chiefly progesterone. Progesterone further prepares the endometrial lining to receive the fertilized egg.

In fact, with pregnancy, the corpus luteum really overworks. It delivers a copious, nonstop production of hormone. This is largely responsible for the very thick, healthy uterine lining that awaits the ovum.

The Egg in the Womb

What happens when the egg arrives in the womb?

I'm sure there must be great rejoicing. Just imagine. The womb has been shedding its lining month in and month out, maybe for years. It does this with monotonous regularity, fully believing that one day it will achieve its purpose in life—receiving a fertilized egg!

I am sure that if humans had any say in the matter, they would give up in sheer disgust and frustration. It's much like a mechanic having an automobile in peak condition on a certain day every month ready for the owner to come and take it on a fierce, marathon drive. But the driver never arrives. This may go on for twenty years or more, month after month. But the mechanic still does his task dutifully. Everything is in peak condition. The fateful day arrives. No driver. But discouragement is never allowed to set in. He must be on the spot for the next appointment.

What takes place when the egg reaches the uterus and all is in readiness for it?

The egg (or morula, as we previously noted it is now technically termed) quickly becomes embedded in the thick, vascular uterine lining.

The outer covering of cells bites into the lining of the womb and very quickly starts absorbing food from the blood vessels there. These cells then develop minute fingerlike projections called villi. They further penetrate into the lining. Very rapidly an active circulation is established between the cell mass and the uterine lining.

What's happening to the prospective baby all this time?

The inner part of the cell mass continues to divide and redivide. Very quickly the cells start to differentiate out into the basic organs of the forthcoming infant. Before long a recognizable fetus is formed.

As the various parts develop, the sac containing it swells up and fills with a special fluid. For the ensuing nine months, until the time it is born, the baby is literally swimming in a sac of fluid.

Growth Rate and Birth

How quickly does the baby grow?

The infant develops quickly. By the end of the third month it is about 9 cm (3¹/₂ in) in length from crown to heel.

By the fourth month it has grown to 15 cm (6 in) and weighs about four ounces.

By the fifth month it is 22 cm (8¹/₂ in) long and weighs about 225 grams (half a pound). By the sixth month it is 30 cm (12 in) long, and weighs about 675 grams (1.5 lb).

By the seventh month, it measures 35 cm (14 in) from crown to heel, and weighs in at 1.1 kg (2¹/₂ lb). By the eighth month it measures 40 cm (16 in) and weighs around 1.6 kg (3¹/₂ lb). By the ninth month it is 45 cm (18 in) long and weighs 2 kg (4¹/₂ lb). By the end of the tenth lunar month (which equals 40 weeks, the total time of conception) it has reached its final birth length of 50 cm (20 in) and weighs around 3.4 kg (7¹/₂ lb).

Various methods are used to determine the growth rate of the infant. However, from a practical point of view, the LMP and EDC system together with the appearance of the mother's abdomen is the usual and simplest way.

What do all these letters mean?

The LMP means "last menstrual period." As we do not know for certain the moment conception takes place, it is simpler to estimate dates from the first day of the last normal menstrual period. This is called the "menstruation-labor interval." This interval is commonly regarded as 280 days, or 40 weeks, or ten lunar months.

Physicians often consult specially prepared tables which set out the LMP and underneath the EDC, which is short for "estimated date of confinement."

A simple way to calculate this date is to add ten days to the first day of the LMP and then count back three months. For example, if the LMP was June 3, then the EDC is March 13. (June 3 plus 10 equals June 13. Count back 3 months equals March 13 of the following year.)

The Placenta

How is the baby actually nourished during its growth in the womb?

The growing fetus is attached by a lifeline termed the umbilical cord to the placenta. The placenta is the area which became attached to the womb lining at the time the fertilized egg entered the uterus. Fairly rapidly the cells of the uterine lining and the cells from the adjacent egg mass become intertwined. Maternal blood, and blood from the developing fetus come into close proximity. Indeed, in later pregnancy they are separated only by a very thin membrane.

Food, vitamins, and the chemicals necessary for life and growth diffuse across this fine membrane and are absorbed by the fetus. Conversely, the waste products from the infant are carried back via blood vessels in the umbilical cord and are expelled into the maternal blood circulation and later voided by the mother.

What ultimately happens to the placenta and other unwanted products in the womb once the baby is born?

The placenta is a large meaty-looking mass of tissue. Once the baby is born it is of no further use.

Soon after the delivery, this is expelled by the uterus. It is called the third stage, or afterbirth.

Obstetricians are very fussy to make certain the entire

afterbirth comes away after the actual birth. Unless this takes place, severe hemorrhages from the womb can occur. These are called postpartum hemorrhages and can be alarming because of the volume of blood that can be lost within seconds.

These days, with careful obstetrics, availability of blood, care in blood typing, and being prepared· for all such emergencies, disasters are not so common as they once were with these sudden emergencies.

In most medical universities a student sitting for his final examinations will be failed instantly if he does not know the treatment of a sudden postpartum hemorrhage.

Are more babies born at night than during daytime?

It's an age-old belief that more are born between the hours of sunset and sunrise than during daylight hours. In fact, a few years ago an Australian doctor carried out a statistical analysis. In a series of 2654 consecutive births at a Sydney obstetrics hospital, 1446 births (54.5 percent) occurred between 9 pm and 9 am.

The remainder, 1208 (45.5 percent), occurred bewteen 9 am and 9 pm. That means that 19 percent more births occurred at night.

The busiest hour was between 1 am and 2 am. Most baggy-eyed, sleep-deprived obstetricians would readily testify to the accuracy of these figures, I am sure.

Another unrelated observation this same doctor made was the comparatively small number that were born during meal hours. However, once born, babies are not so well known for their choice of habits or their concern for others.

The Developing Fetus

You said earlier that the age of the developing infant can be roughly estimated by feeling the mother's abdomen?

Yes. This gives a rough idea of the stage she has reached in the confinement calendar. It is spoken of by the obstetrician as the height of the fundus.

The fundus is the base of the uterus. As the infant develops within this organ, it gradually increases in size, and progressively rises up into the abdominal cavity.

At sixteen weeks the base can be felt just above the symphisis pubis, the bones that form the front part of the pelvic girdle. (This bone may be easily felt in the general area of the pubic hair.)

At twenty-four weeks the fundus has reached the level of the umbilicus (or navel).

At thirty-six weeks it has reached the lower margin of the breast-bone.

At forty weeks just before birth is due, the fundus drops a little and is located just below the end of the breast-bone.

Signs and Tests for Pregnancy

What are some of the early signs of pregnancy?

The chief and commonest sign is a sudden cessation of normal menstruation.

Certainly many factors can cause this. Nervous upsets are well known for their ability at playing unkind pranks. However, in a woman with normal, regular periods who indulges in regular intercourse, the chances of pregnancy being the cause for the amenorrhea (as this is technically called) are high.

Morning sickness is another telltale sign. This usually puts in an appearance at six weeks, and may continue until the end of the third month. It is more common with first babies. There may be vomiting, but usually it's a sensation of nausea rather than lack of appetite.

If this nausea is troublesome, special tablets are now widely available which give rapid and almost magical relief.

There is often a desire to pass the urine more often than normal. This is due to the enlarging mass in the pelvic region and its pressure on the bladder.

Breast changes start early and are usually noticeable in the second and third months. Superficial veins become more prominent, the breasts firm up, and the area about the nipples becomes a darker color. Often tiny glands in the area surrounding the nipples stand out prominently. Sometimes a clear fluid comes from the nipples themselves.

Changes in the size and shape of the uterus occur. A physician experienced in examining pregnant wombs can usually detect this after six or eight weeks.

What is the accuracy of pregnancy tests?

Pregnancy testing has undergone marked changes over the past few years.

Once it was a time-consuming process. The test was originally carried out on white mice. It was called the AZR test (being short for Ascheim-Zondek Reaction). Later toads were used. The urine from a supposedly pregnant woman was injected into the animal, and 100 hours later the mouse was killed and its ovaries examined. If a corpus luteum was discovered, this was diagnostic of pregnancy.

However, physicians now use the simple chemical immunological tests. Within three minutes it is possible to give an accurate answer as to whether or not a woman is pregnant. Even in early pregnancy (from about eight weeks on) a chemical hormone called chorionic gonadotrophin is produced by the developing placenta. Some of this finds its way into the mothers's urine. It can be quickly detected by the relatively simple screening tests.

Now this has entirely replaced the older tests that required pathologists keeping cages full of white mice or green toads, and spending hours of valuable time on testing.

A Wonderful Experience or—

I suppose that wraps up the pregnancy story. Do you have any final comments?

Just one or two. Pregnancy and reproduction are about the greatest events that will ever befall a woman. It is a wonderful, almost magical, situation. Under the right circumstances it can be a happy event. But under adverse circumstances, it can be a mentally frustrating, almost paralyzing situation.

Pregnancy is physically possible in women from the age of puberty onward; but many years usually pass before the average girl is socially and economically equipped to reproduce. It's worth waiting until then. Don't play with fire before you have married and established your own home. The payoff for those who wait and do it the sensible, preplanned way is tremendous.

Unplanned, unwanted pregnancies, particularly in those not yet married, can only spell dismay, doom, and disaster. I have seen it happen too often to believe otherwise. Be careful as you progress through the early years of your life. Be sensible. Stick to the high moral code that guarantees the perfect result and the happiest situation.

All About Dates

What's your opinion on the dating system?

I believe it's not only a good system, but an essential one. However, "the system" covers a tremendously broad spectrum of activities. It needs a bit of qualifying.

How do you mean?

Reduced to its basic ingredients, this is what is generally mentally conjectured when we talk of dating:

1. Boy meets girl.
2. Boy is attracted to girl.
3. Boy makes effort to make himself attractive to girl. Therefore, he takes her out, buys her gifts, extends his personality to complete the conquest.
4. Girl is attracted to boy and responds to his efforts.
5. Couple become engaged, later married, and live happily ever after.

That sounds a bit like the Hollywood version.

Not really. Take any two kids and multiply this by a few million, and this is the basic routine.

It's the social custom of the Western world. Maybe it's good, maybe it's not. Who is to say? However, when you compare it with some of the other possibilities, most couples would say it's preferable.

The custom in some lands is for the parents to make the choice as to whom their children should marry. This is often arranged when the children are born or very early in their life.

Just imagine having no say in whom your life partner is destined to be. It could be "X," a person you find intolerable and revolting!

I suppose some married couples will claim that this has happened to them in any case. Even when they were given freedom of choice!

Very definitely so. But in point of fact the fault has been their own. They have either made a false choice in the first instance or they failed to follow some of the basic requirements to make their marriage happy and successful.

At what age should dating commence?

It is impossible to lay down hard and fast rules and to fix dogmatically age ranges for this phenomenon.

In a sense, in its very broadest application, "dating" should commence at a very early age.

By this I mean it's healthy and desirable for boys and girls to associate freely from the time they are babies and upward. The greater (and the earlier) the intermingling of the two sexes the better. There is no doubt in my mind that families that have both boys and girls have fewer problems later on in life when more substantial boy-girl relationships are being formed. Similarly, it often seems that children attending coeducational schools fall into a similar category. By frequent association with members of the opposite sex a closer understanding of each other develops. What more happy, healthful way than during the important formative years of life?

In this age stratum things seem more natural than in later

years when inner conflicts and personality problems tend to loom and cloud the issue.

The Case of Jerry's Nose

Can you give a few specific details to clarify your meaning?

Certainly. We often consult with growing teen-agers. It is common to see them with a whole heap of problems.

For example, I well remember Jerry, a reasonably happy seventeen-year-old boy. He was one of four boys in this particular family. There were no sisters, and Jerry had attended a boys' high school. On this particular day Jerry had come to see me about, of all strange things, his nose. There was a small bump in the center of it.

I am well aware that thousands of people have slightly irregular nasal structures. Furthermore, many are perplexed by this, and many take positive steps to have their particular problem rectified.

But in Jerry's case it was not very obvious to me and certainly did not seem to warrant the importance he was attaching to it right then. His chief request was that I refer him to a plastic surgeon who would remove the bump and make him normal.

I was a bit intrigued by this request and felt there was something more to it than appeared at first sight. A bit of gentle prodding soon produced the answer loud and clear: To this point in his life Jerry had not possessed the courage to speak to anyone of the opposite sex.

His entire life has been a male-oriented one. There were no sisters. He had attended a boys' school and had seldom met girls on anything more than rare and very superficial lines.

Now that he was growing up, and his hormones had started careering around his system, he had felt the inner stirrings that come to all red-blooded, normal humans. He felt the inner desire and need to make contact with his female counterparts. But he lacked the inner know-how.

The more he watched his contemporaries make the grade, the more frustrated he felt. He started to feel insecure, unsure of himself, irritated and agitated. Finally, as he looked at himself in the mirror, he unconsciously sought basic reasons for his apparent failure. He happened to notice the small lump in the middle of his nose and decided this was the real reason he could not "get along with women," as he put it. He used this as the whipping boy, you might say. Finally, he attributed to his nose the fact that women looked at him once and then rejected him because he was abnormal or some sort of human freak!

It all sounds a bit way out, don't you think?

Way out maybe to you or to me and to others. But not to Jerry. It was very real. He was accepting this as an escape mechanism. If he had something physical to blame, it gave him a mental escape and so helped to preserve what was left of his manliness and personality.

The Case of Marcelle

Do you believe that with a different home and school environment Jerry would have grown up differently?

I feel there is little doubt about it. Take Marcelle, for example. She too came from a family of four. In her case there were two boys and two girls forming the family unit. Being the eldest, she had her share of home duties to carry out right from a very early age. She'd helped care for the younger ones as they came along. She'd assisted her mother in bathing, feeding, dressing, and entertaining them one by one as the years came and went.

When she went to school, she fitted into the boy-girl associations which in her mind were merely an extension of homelife.

Her ease and poise with boys was similar to her attitude to girls. She felt at home. There was no sense of being ill at ease. In fact, for many years she regarded boys as rather stupid characters who needed a little mothering. This was a direct result of her position at home.

What was the final outcome in her case?

As time went by, she was friendly with many boys. In fact, for a long time she did not have "dates" with any specific boy, but rather preferred group outings and social gatherings. When specific friendships did begin to form, she already had a well-tried yardstick by which to measure them. She finally married a likable fellow from her home church, and a happy home has been established.

Marcelle is now a mother of two fine children herself. I am sure the future of this household is assured.

But What About Boys Like Jerry?

Now this sounds just great, and I go along with your views. But aren't you dooming the many unlucky people who happen to fall into Jerry's category? What happens to them? Are they doomed to eternal sadness and inferiority complexes?

Not really. My basic plan in telling these two little stories (which happen to be true in all details) is this: The importance of early, persisting interrelationship with the opposite sex really does pay off as time goes by. By coming to associate freely with your contemporaries, barriers are not set up in the first place. This means they don't have to be broken down later. When I say "barriers," I am referring to such traits as shyness, feeling insecure, not knowing how to make contact with others, feeling awkward and gawky, being tongue-tied when it matters most.

It is essential that boys and girls recognize their contemporaries on an equal plane. We are all together in this world. If you suddenly elevate Jim to a higher level in your mind, you immediately start to erect mental barriers. This means you are destined to feel inferior (again in your own mind) when you contact him. When the barriers are present, you're guaranteed to initiate problems along the lines we've mentioned. Early, free association certainly helps to prevent this.

Please, I must know what eventuated with Jerry.

In the case of Jerry, once it became obvious what the basic problem was, it was then a matter of reeducation. I suggested we postpone the surgical attack on his nose for a while. Instead, we decided to embark on some mental surgery.

Bit by bit (over the next few weeks) we went through his past history. We pieced together the story as to why his nose was bothering him. This in turn revealed his hidden complexes. Very soon we embarked on a line of positive thinking. Jerry was given a definite routine to follow.

If the famous Broadway star of yesteryear, Jimmy Durante, could make the world laugh at his hideous nose (and make a million dollars and thousands of friends beside), surely there was hope for our Jerry.

Very quickly Jerry came to realize that his problems were basically not in his nose but a bit deeper placed—in his mind.

Although his early boy-girl relationships had been sparse, emphasis was placed on the future. Jerry was mentally alert and sensible in his activities. His grades were good, and his potential for the future was excellent.

There was no reason in the world why he should feel at a loss with girls. I helped him adopt a positive philosophy: "I am a normal, happy, healthy individual. I am making good headway in the world. I am as good as the other fellow. In fact, according to my reports, I am better than the average other fellow. My nose is quite normal. I want to get to know my contemporaries, especially female companions, and from this point on I am determined I shall.''

What was the outcome from all this?

Within a few months Jerry had certainly come to know a wide circle of people. He started to move around with more confidence. People started to like him. Those he'd known but casually came to be his very good friends. Soon he was dating various young ladies, and before long he had come to form a special friendship with one very attractive girl.

Jerry is a completely different person now. As I tell this story, he is engaged and plans to marry in a few months' time. The girl of his choice is a bright, cheery girl, and I am convinced that she is the right girl for him. I have every confidence that they will establish a happy, lasting home equal to that of Marcelle.

I am relieved to hear the happy outcome. For a while I was a little concerned and feared the worst for Jerry! One might say that his problems were essentially all in the mind.

Exactly. Most problems are, but by carefully routing them out, they can be eliminated forever. However, it takes time, persistence, patience, but above all the recognition of the fact that they exist in the first instance.

If Jerry had not come along with his nose problem, it is quite likely he'd have gone on nurturing his inner conflicts forever. Under these circumstances I'm sure his future happiness would have been in serious jeopardy.

Hormones and the Teen-ager

Earlier we spoke about the age dating could start. You've pointed out some of the basic essentials that make for easier boy-girl relationships as they advance in years. Are there other elements that affect the age-of-dating system?

There certainly are. In fact, there are scores of factors that affect this. Some growing teen-agers are well developed mentally and physically at the age of fifteen. In other instances, a contemporary will not mature to this extent until he or she has reached seventeen or eighteen years or even older. Indeed, some persons are still mentally underdeveloped right throughout life! (Just look about and you'll soon see what I mean. I am not talking about the mentally defective, but just apparently normal people who have failed to mature mentally.)

Is there any control over all this from the point of view of the individual?

This entire question is basically in the hands of nature, the unseen influence that guides our development. Much of the time we have only a limited control over our inner physical structure. As we discussed earlier, the factors governing our emotional makeup are in fact chemical reactions. The chemicals are called hormones. They are produced both by male and female. Everyone has some of each. But in females the female chemicals or hormones predominate. In males it is the reverse; male chemicals predominate.

The chemical factories which produce these products are not very active in the early years of life. But when the age of puberty arrives, wonderful changes occur. Suddenly, the *secondary sex characteristics* take hold of the system. The factors we recognize as physcial and mental adult development take place.

And over this we have no control?

That is correct. It stems from within. There is a certain amount of heredity involved. That means that if your parents "matured" early, then you will also, in all probability. And vice versa.

Also, we know from actual experience that persons in

more so-called "civilized" countries (the parts we know as the Western world) tend to develop more rapidly and at a substantially earlier age than other races. Nobody is quite sure why this occurs. It may be tied in with the more hectic pace of living prevalent in the modern hurly-burly world we know. Maybe it's the stringent emphasis placed in sticking to time schedules; to the emphasis on sex in our world, and to various other unknown factors.

But irrespective of age, as soon as the hormones start moving about the system, doesn't that have a wonderful effect on the inner emotions?

Very definitely. The mental changes following puberty are marked. As greater and increasingly greater quantities of hormones are produced, so the strong attraction of the sexes starts. Over this, as well, we have no basic control. It will happen, come what may.

Dating and Mating

Then you'd say that our inherent physiology guarantees that sooner or later boys and girls must get around to this phenomenon known as dating?

Dating *and* mating. For sure! With some, the urges will come earlier than with others. In some they will be modest, and not very marked for a number of years. But in others again, they will be surging, fiery, demanding, dominant. For this reason it is not possible to give actual ages at which the dating system is reasonable. It varies with each individual.

No doubt there are other factors involved as well.

As I said before, various factors are involved. The early home upbringing certainly plays a part. Where boy-girl relations have been occurring on a normal plane since birth, there is often not the same overwhelming interest in the opposite sex when the hormones start their earliest rumblings.

With late development, and a mild hormonal production, there may also not be such a lavish interest on the male section of the species for a few more years.

Often the attitude of the parents which manifests itself to a large extent in the child's attitudes to life in general comes through at this stage also. Many children with the mid-Victorian upbringing which teaches that anything to do with the opposite sex is wicked, evil, and sinful are also likely to become involved in opposite attractions a bit later than their contemporaries.

I firmly believe that this sort of upbringing is fraught only with potential dangers. So often have I seen youngsters subjected to this early type of education. All goes well for a time. Then suddenly at a later-than-normal age they realize that they possess a built-in hormonal system. Bang! It goes off overnight. The parental oppression (for want of a better word) is suddenly spurned, the growing adult discovers that his or her upbringing has been abnormally suppressed, and major problems loom.

What is the answer to this?

The answer, of course, is for parents to take a sensible middle-of-the-road course. Undue, abnormal suppression of growing youth is foolish. It must and will finally burst out uncontrolled. It is only a matter of time.

Just the same, a reasonably strict childhood upbringing is essential. Growing youth (as growing youth will agree) cannot be given an entirely free rein. Cooperative, sensible unity of thought is the basic ideal. This certainly can occur.

True Love

Do you believe there is such a thing as "true love" involved in dating?

I believe that a sincere feeling between two persons can

occur. But this is certainly not akin to true love in the full sense of the word. True love, I am convinced, can come only after many years of happy, harmonious married life.

But thousands of youngsters firmly believe they are deeply in love.

To be sure, they do. And I am certain that they are quite sincere in their belief that they are actually in love. But in the stormy developing years, the distinction between true "love" and sexual "infatuation" is hard for a growing mind to distinguish. The turbulent surging effect of the sex hormones creates in all maturing people a tremendous desire for the admiration and association of the opposite sex. It cannot be otherwise. Nature has designed it this way.

This sexual attraction often blinds individuals to everything else. Because they are attracted emotionally to another person, they instantly believe that they are in love.

Then how does one know whether the attraction is only a youthful infatuation or genuine love?

I believe it is tremendously difficult to tell. The younger the age, the harder it is. I believe that for every year under the age of twenty-one years, the greater is the difficulty, and the more likely one is to make an error of personal judgment.

Are you suggesting then that persons under twenty-one years should not date?

Certainly not. But I feel that it requires extremely careful assessment of all factors before couples under twenty-one embark on married life.

Over the years I have witnessed so many under-twenty-one marriages fall to pieces after a short time that I now view any such union with suspicion and disquiet.

The changes that take place in one's mental processes, their outlook and inner feelings during the "twenties" are in some respects almost as marked as those that occur during puberty. Many people (in fact I would say the majority) do not mature emotionally until their twenties.

I am sure there is nothing worse than being united forever to a person with whom there is incompatibility.

"Act in haste, repent at leisure" is a good, old-time slogan that's been bandied around for many years. Yet, to my mind, it is just as true today as it was when first coined by some observant philosopher. The number of youthful marriages that wind up as sad, unhappy unions and ultimately "fall to pieces" would fill a library of registers. Who wants to be among them?

In Love Under Twenty-one?

Let's get back to the question of being "in love" when under this arbitrary age of twenty-one. I am sure that the day you turn twenty-one there is no sudden, magical change in your outlook.

There is not. But as the years tick by, a gradual alteration in outlook and judgment takes place. After being around for twenty-one years, a person has gleaned a lot of knowledge. (I am sorry to say that most have not accumulated as much as they think they have, however!)

At this age they are in a better position to make sensible decisions. For sure, many errors of judgment will occur. But the gross number will be fewer. In the overall picture the chances of error are substantially less.

Let's pursue the thought a little bit further. I've seen many youngsters marry at early ages such as sixteen, seventeen, or eighteen years. Some of these marriages succeed, but most do not.

Again, I have also seen many take place in the ages beyond twenty-one. For example, twenty-two, twenty-four, twenty-seven and thirty. I would say from personal observation that a greater proportion of marriages occurring with this older, more mature group tend to hold together more firmly and to last longer than any of the other younger groups.

Do you believe there is a basic reason for this?

Of course there is. With another round of experience in this world (being subject to people, the rigors of living, the perplexities of life), people can form more mature, more sensible decisions. Judgment is keener. It is easier to judge personalities more readily and more accurately.

At an older age a person knows what he wants in life. He knows the type of person he wishes to have as a partner. He is not so involved with superficial features. He will more likely search deeper and dig out the factors which are lasting.

Good looks are lovely, to be sure. But we all know that these are only skin deep. Personality, grace and charm, a specific educational status, consistency of manner, common sense—these all suddenly loom as more important factors than a shapely figure.

Men are easily duped in early life. Many of them are in later life also. But the majority realize, after a while, that gorgeous shapes have little to do with lasting values. So as time progresses, these start to assume progressively reduced importance in their eyes. This is definitely worth remembering.

Hints for Dating

What about a few general points to sum up your views on the dating system?

I feel it could be summarized as follows:

1. Dating is tremendously important in the life of every growing young person.

2. The age it should start varies with everyone. It depends on the physical and mental maturity of the persons involved. (This, in turn, is largely governed by one's inner physical

development and hormonal production.)

3. Do not forget that you're not odd if you don't suddenly start dating. Often there is lots more fun in "going with the group" rather than pairing off as couples. I believe that in the early years it is certainly a better idea to get around with the crowd, and enjoy group friendship (boys and girls together) than to slink off in couple formation. (The latter will come soon enough.)

4. As all this is taking place when the chemical production of the body is running high, it is definitely safer to "go with the crowd" in the early years. It is so easy to "get involved" when stowed away as a lonesome twosome. Hidden dangers can easily get out of hand. (We'll talk more about this later on.)

5. Those with mixed family backgrounds (ie, both boys and girls in the family unit) are likely to have less adjustment problems when boy-girl relationships are becoming established. But this does not mean that failure is the fate of all others. It is largely in the hands of the individual. Positive thinking, and taking definite steps in this direction, will undoubtedly save the day (and the friend) every time.

6. Growing youth frequently accepts sexual attraction (or "infatuation") with the opposite sex as being "in love." It is not, and should be carefully considered, especially if there is any question of marriage involved.

7. The older the person, the more mature and sensible the judgment is likely to be. Marriages entered into under the age of twenty-one can often breed problems. Those embarked upon after this age generally are more likely to succeed, merely because the couples are more mature in thought and judgment. They also know what they want in life and can seek a partner who will help them to this end.

8. If you have any query on your feelings, it's not a bad idea

to discuss it with your parents. Don't forget that your problems of today were their problems of yesteryear. They went through identical situations. When the crunch is on, most parents are happy to help solve your problems too, irrespective of what they are.

9. Also, it is a good idea to enlist the power of prayer to God, especially when important decisions must be made. The best time is at night before you go to bed. It is surprising how loudly and clearly the answer comes through. Often by next morning you have the answer well in hand. It's a method I've used for years with problems covering many aspects of life. It even works with boy-girl relations, irrespective of the age group you presently come under. Use it, and use it often.

Going Steady

A natural sequel to the idea of "Dates and All That" is our next item: "Going Steady." What is your definition of this?

In my mind there is little doubt as to what it means. I take it that some years have elapsed now in the life of our typical young miss. The person involved has been growing, maturing mentally and physically. She has been through the dating system. I hope she has been around with groups for some years, developed lots of friends on a general plane, and discovered the intrinsic pleasures of knowing many people. You know, there are few pleasures akin to knowing people and developing friends in the wide definition of the word. Friends acquired in early life frequently last you for the rest of your life. It is well known that the older we become the fewer friends we tend to make. Maybe we haven't so much time. Maybe we (and they) are not so outreaching with ourselves and our personalities. But attachments made during the younger years are often kept for decades.

I'm not necessarily referring to close ties but friends in general. For this reason I attach great importance to youngsters in their teens coming to know as many people (particularly their contemporaries) as they can. It's essential they become friends with members of both sexes. There are few things as pleasing as to dig up old friends in later life. The ones you made early are often the ones that count most later on. (Just mark my words!)

Now after some years of having lots of friends, our young miss has ultimately discovered that one special person is more attractive to her than the others. Therefore, he and she have decided to go along together. In other words they are "going steady."

Do you think most "steadies" actually wind up marrying?

Lots do. Lots do not. It depends on many factors.

But it is at least a sort of trial to see if they really like one another as much as they first believed they did.

Possibly the best thing about "going steady" is the fact that no legal attachment has taken place. Both are still quite free to go their own way if and when they so elect.

Of course, once marriage is entered into, the situation differs enormously. That is forever! Or if it is not forever, it involves a tremendous amount of trouble, cost, headache, and invariably heartache.

We, as Christians, believe "once married, always married." There is only one reason wherein marriage can be legitimately terminated in the eyes of God. I am afraid that if more couples realized this fact, a lot more thought would be given to marriage than is the case at present. I am sure many youngsters would wait for a few more years to pass before they took this vital step as well. It is so permanent!

A jester once said: "Marriage is not a word. It's a sentence." How right this can be! Therefore, as I've been saying to kids madly in love (and literally straining to get to the marriage alter): "Look before you leap." Sensible ones do. Those who just cannot control themselves rush off—

frequently to their eternal regret.

Do you think there are special problems involved when a couple is "going steady"?

Are there ever! I'd say this is when problems really start to soar!

What Happens?

How come?

It's like this. As we explained earlier, the system's hormonal apparatus is geared to make the opposite sexes vitally attractive to each other. This begins at the age of puberty. It very rapidly rises. Some physiologists claim that it can reach its peak in the mid-to-late teens. That means around the ages of sixteen to nineteen years.

Now, just picture the situation in the cold rays of daylight, and you'll see what I mean. Here you have a couple of kids. Each has a really powerful motor inside, just bursting to "get going." At this stage they are not really sure where it's geared to take them. They have vague, general ideas only.

Suddenly they find they're "going steady." In essence this often means they're off somewhere all alone. Just the two of them are there. The two of them, in clandestine darkness, with nothing else but themselves and their thoughts to propel them along.

What happens?

I simply love the naïveté of your questions. I know you're trying to help me explain a very delicate operation. Not a surgical one, but a physical one! Why, I believe this is even more delicate than a surgical operation, in a sense!

I think I said these two kids were there all alone. That's not quite true. You see, nature is there too, lurking in the backdrop. As we've stated before, nature has one and only one intention in mind—propagation of the species. She's mad bent on seeing that the human race doesn't grind to a sudden halt. It seems hardly possible, but just to be certain she is present wherever and whenever youngsters come together—in their two's. Her allies are isolation, darkness, soft music, peace and quietness, and mental relaxation and contentment.

These are the *avant garde* assistants. Assistants she uses whenever possible with deadly cunning. Under these circumstances, with nature and her allies urging at the sideline, quite often the young couple find themselves unable to handle the situation adroitly. Every year millions of youngsters in these young age groups are literally "carried away" by the overwhelmingly violent urges of the moment.

It is so easy to get involved in compromising situations where there is no turning back. Premarital sex is often engaged in to the fullest extent. And let me assure you, when it has happened once, it is likely to occur again. And again and again and again.

At first this may not seem important. But quite apart from the moral issue involved, there is always the danger of an unplanned, unwanted pregnancy.

What then?

I assure you, from many years in the practice of medicine, this is a problem to which there is no ready solution.

Then do you condemn premarital sex?

I certainly believe that youngsters engaging in premarital sex are acting unwisely. Not only is it quite contrary to Christian principles, but the added fears, frustrations, and problems it subsequently generates can develop into giant-sized ogres. An evening's pleasure can give rise to months (and often years) of worry, problems, heartaches, and heartbreaks. Every day or every week I see some youngster who is having problems.

Jan's Story

What about a few stories to illustrate the points?

There are so many it's hard to know which ones to select. Maybe one sample will illustrate what I have in mind.

Jan was a country girl living in another state. I first caught up with her when she came to stay with relatives in my town. She was an attractive seventeen-year-old, still in high school. I knew her relatives well. I guess that was the reason she came to stay with them, and ultimately to see me. By the time I saw her, Jan was about three months pregnant.

Her story was not original. Not new. Not particularly interesting. She was a high school kid who was "going steady" with Jim. Jim had known her for several years. Both had been born and bred in the same small rural town. Jim was two years older than Jan. He'd quit school earlier, got himself a job, bought a fast car, and bored through his weekly earnings at a faster rate than he earned them.

The car, it seems, had been the cause of their downfall. There were a few unsupervised late nights, no doubt parked someplace where there were no passersby. In a rural town this would not be difficult. Suddenly Jan realized "something was wrong." A subsequent pregnancy test gave the result: "Positive." Jan was very definitely pregnant by the time she had the courage to face up and tell her parents. They were reasonable people. But they hadn't condoned the friendship, realizing that Jim's fast ways, love of fast cars, and lack of thought for finances and the basics of life could lead to trouble later on.

In a small town gossip travels faster than the telegraph. Jan had been very keen to become a nurse. In fact, it had been a lifelong dream. The two stark alternatives that faced her now were: (a) Marry Jim and legalize the whole thing. Although Jan liked Jim to the point of being his "steady," deep down she often wondered if he really was the man for her. There was doubt, insecurity deep down, no real true basic love. Possibility (b): Get "something" done. The "something" of course was either an abortion or having the child and adopting it out. Both seemed to Jan and her parents a national disaster at that moment.

But one factor was absolutely certain. A decision one way or the other had to be made quickly. There remained only a matter of months before the baby was due to arrive, come what may! There were no grounds for legal termination of pregnancy, and in her state the laws about this were tight and almost insuperable. It was a criminal offense for anyone carrying out such a procedure, as well as for the patient. Therefore, whatever her moral views, this was out for practical purposes.

Jan reluctantly decided on the other line. She decided to continue with the pregnancy, give birth to the infant, and arrange an "at birth" adoption. Fortunately for her, she had good friends in another state. Therefore, it was relatively simple for her to arrange an interstate "holiday."

When the time to go actually arrived, there was a lot of heart tugging. Leaving home at the age of seventeen is not everyone's idea of happiness. Going away under these circumstances it was even worse. At this point Jan realized for the hundredth time that maybe "chastity does pay." (I might add that right now she's absolutely certain of the fact.)

Soon after the pregnancy had been confirmed, Jim seemed to lose interest in the entire deal. Although there had been vague promises of financial assistance at the time, these also became more and more vague as the date for Jan's departure neared.

Finally, when the crunch came, there was no further sign of Jim, or his fast car, or of any monetary help.

Like so many millions of similar promises made under such circumstances, they disappeared like the morning mists—and about as rapidly. This did not do much to improve Jan's mental frame of mind at the time.

Anyhow, Jan left home, came to town, and moved in with her relatives. I saw her shortly after and went ahead and made full arrangements. I have a standing arrangement with a nearby hospital for cases such as this. They are very kind and give young mothers in distress every possible assistance. In fact, I think they are too kind at times.

The routine was for me to take care of the pregnancy for the next several months. She would stay with the relatives. When it was time for the baby to appear, she would enter the hospital in the usual fashion, and at birth the baby would immediately be adopted out to some kind, deserving couple.

In fact, Jan was destined never to see her little one. The pregnancy proceeded normally. One would expect it to, for Jan was a healthy country girl with no history of any illness. The confinement swept along as planned. There were no labor complications. Everything was perfect. The adopting parents assumed responsibility for the child. The baby was a delight that would bring joy to any mother's heart and light to the eye.

But such mental rewards were not for Jan. Indeed, the days she spent in the hospital following the birth were ones filled with a terrible gloom.

While adjacent mothers suckled their newborn babes and bathed them and tended to them with all the joy and serenity that only motherhood can impart, Jan was minus hers. She knew the reason why and knew it could be no other way. But that did not lessen the tearing pangs that seared their way through her heart like a bayonet would many times a day.

The cry of a baby immediately set her on edge. It might be

"her baby." How was she to know? In fact, how was she ever to know if her own flesh and blood was being treated kindly by the new parents or maliciously abused or mal-treated? These thoughts continually circulated and recirculated through her mind day after day.

I well remember visiting Jan on my morning ward rounds one day.

"What does she look like, doctor?" she asked, her voice low and filled with a tender passion. "Is she pretty? Does she have blue eyes? I have blue eyes, and I hope she has too. I've called her Marea. I had a doll I loved and called it Marea, and I want my baby to have the same name—"

At that point Jan broke down completely and wept until I thought there could be no more tears left in her small body.

"Marea will be well cared for, Jan." I tried to soothe the sad, sorrowing mother. "It's all for the best. God will look after your little one, I am sure. Time will heal the sad wounds."

But no words of solace could lessen the surging feelings of her tortured brain. In fact, I fully believe that, right then, the death of her little one might have been preferable to Jan to the sort of twisting agony she was enduring.

Jan's depression worsened over the next few days. "Post-natal blues" are well known in maternal circles. No one is quite sure what initiates them. But added to this was the mental perplexity that Jan was trying to hide. Here she was, a stranger, virtually, in a strange town, paying the heavy penalty for a few foolish moments of lustful "lovemaking." Here was the end result of a youngster "going steady," but who (like so many others) found the pace a little too hectic, the temptations a little too hard to endure. Nature had certainly won out. The payoff was not worth the candy.

What eventually became of Jan?

I had to get my psychiatric colleague to visit her and give her special treatment. He was quite convinced that the emotional upset had been too much for her to take. However, with sympathy and understanding and good nursing, she made the grade. She was finally discharged (all alone) and eventually went back to her rural hometown.

Jan finally married another young man from the same town. But I am sure she was a much wiser young lady after this nerve-racking, soul-destroying, maternally upsetting event than before.

Maybe the story of Jan (again a true story) may help guide someone reading this book today. I hope it does.

The moral, of course, is obvious. "Going steady" is quite OK. But it does present a special set of problems. Never, *never* underestimate the power of your built-in motor system. Once it starts, it is often virtually impossible to turn it off. The final payoff can be a soul-shattering one, to say the least.

"Petting" and "Heavy Petting"

But when couples go steady, there must be many normal situations which are quite innocuous. Surely the sex bogey does not rear up every time.

Quite right. Couples can have lots and lots of fun together. They can go places, visit here and there, engage in sport, picnics, outings. But sooner or later problem situations are bound to arise. The sex attractions must come to the surface ultimately.

These go by all sorts of names: Necking, petting, and other words eminently describe what commences as innocent boy-girl relations.

Of course, the crunch is that one thing leads to another. Holding hands is merely an early sign of sexual attraction. In itself, this is perfectly harmless. However, when embarked on for the first time, it can cause a few missed heartbeats. It can cause the adrenalin of the system to be pumped out in greater-than-normal quantities.

The incident is attractive. It spells nearness, being wanted, a sort of mystical union between two persons. It is also a bit like a drug of addiction. It's so good that more is desired. And just as with drugs, the more that is received, the more it is desired. There is seemingly no end.

In addition there is the bonus extra that each time something is acquired, it is not quite so exciting the next time. Therefore, next time there must be a bit more. So simply holding hands steadily develops into more advanced manifestations of sexuality.

Arms around waists doesn't cast much of a spell after the first few times either. There is the natural progression of more and more physical contact. Hugging, cuddling, kissing are all expressions of this great desire to be close.

"The nearer you are to one another, the more sense-stimulating the result," is the general theme of the love-making game.

These expressions go by all manner of names. "Petting" is perhaps a good word to embrace them all in one. There is ordinary petting, and then there is what is known as "heavy petting."

Well, what is heavy petting?

This is the most dangerous form of petting. It's not dangerous in the true sense of the word, in that there is no danger of your life.

In one sense, that is. Yet in another sense there is. It means petting to the extent that both partners become very involved emotionally—almost to the extent of engaging in complete sexual union.

Would you care to be more explicit? After all, we're

writing for a mature, emancipated readership, and we might as well know the exact facts of the situation. I feel that this is vitally important.

I sincerely agree. I think everyone is aware that there are various areas of the body's surface anatomy that are particularly sensitive to stimulation. In women this encompasses the lips, ears, the breast areas, especially the nipples and areas immediately surrounding these. This is termed the areola.

In addition the inner parts of the thighs are extremely sensitive to tactile stimulation. However, the part of the highest sensibility is the little organ named the clitoris. We spoke of this earlier when dealing with the structure of the female pelvic system.

This small organ is located just above the front passageway (vagina), where the two smaller folds (labia minor) guarding the vaginal entrance, unite above. Here millions and millions of nerve endings are located. During times of emotional and tactile stimulation this small organ becomes congested with blood, and tends to enlarge in size. As well, its sensitivity increases many times over.

Like everything else in the human reproductive system, it again is part of nature's up-to-date and clever system of ensuring that reproduction will go on unabated. The fact is that when this is stimulated, there is an almost uncontrollable desire to engage in actual sexual intercourse. A surging desire encompasses the entire female frame. She not only desires it, but becomes eager in her efforts to gain this end product.

The small glands at the entrance to the vagina suddenly produce appreciable amounts of a thickish fluid. This is aimed at lubricating the canal to make intercourse more easy.

Her mind tends to go into a state of "daydream-itis." There is absolutely no doubt that at this stage she is not thinking clearly. This is when her barricades are definitely down. This is when danger lurks. This is the time at which she is likely to lose her self-control. Unfortunately, it is so often the time when she also loses her virginity, as well as her self-esteem.

Boyfriends are often overzealous in taking advantage of this state of affairs. The "smooth operators" are well aware of the methods of stimulating their "steadies." They are there ready, willing, and able to engage in intercourse as soon as there is any indication of willingness on the part of their girl friends.

Aren't there times during the monthly cycle that are especially prone to produce problems?

Yes. During the first half of the menstrual cycle, certain hormones have been quietly building up in the system. By the approximate midpoint of the cycle these are present in superabundance in the system.

This has the effect of making the girl more inclined than ever to be responsive to sexually oriented advances. It really increases her libido (as the clinicians say in their cold, calculating, technical words).

However, the dangerous payoff with sex at this point is the greatly enhanced probability of pregnancy. At this particular time the tiny female egg (ovum) has been released from the ovary and is making its way gingerly down the fallopian tubes en route to the uterus. It is looking eagerly for a male cell with which to unite. This is the time of major emotional internal upheaval. Should the ovum find a sperm (or vice versa), prompt union will take place and a pregnancy is immediately on the way. There is great rejoicing in the uterus itself. At long last the great day for which it has been preparing and planning every month since puberty has finally arrived. But from the point of view of the individual concerned, it is indeed a sorry, sad day.

Sorry, that is, if the couple haven't been united in legal and holy matrimony!

Quite right. But alternatively, if they are married, and have established a home, this day could be one of the greatest in their entire lives.

As I've noticed without fail over the years, the announcement to a happy married couple that the wife is pregnant almost invariably brings great joy. Indeed, the arrival of the first child is an event of a lifetime. There is absolutely nothing in life that can compare with it. But under different circumstances it can be a day of sadness, dismay, and near tragedy so often.

So the basic danger of heavy petting in unmarrieds is the high chance that it will lead on to sexual intercourse and in turn the probability of pregnancy.

In a nutshell, that is the score.

But today with the universal availability of the Pill, as well as other simple methods of contraception, this greatly reduces the problems of possible pregnancies.

You are quite right. However, experience proves that many girls become pregnant on the very first time they engage in unplanned intercourse.

What started out to be a pleasant day at the beach, for example, winds up just that, plus a bit extra. The "bit extra" was the heavy-petting, lovemaking session in the back seat of the boyfriend's car en route for home after the happy day surfing.

Taken unawares, with her defenses and barriers down, many a girl has not even considered the remote possibility of what can (and often does) take place.

Usually, we find that the girls who engage persistently and unashamedly in lustful sex wherever and whenever the opportunity occurs are the ones that run into trouble less often.

The experienced ones (as you might describe them) are on the Pill and have been so for years past.

Although many doctors will not prescribe the Pill to minors, or individuals not obviously married, it is still quite simple for a girl to secure supplies if she really sets her mind at it.

Desire in Males

Do males have a cyclical sex desire factor like women?

No. Males are far more easily aroused sexually than women. They do not have any monthly cyclical waxing and waning. Right from the time of puberty their sex urges really race ahead at breakneck speed.

Many males reach full adult maturity at a relatively early age. At this point they are quite capable of fathering offspring. In fact, some physiology experts claim that many males reach their peak of maturity at the age of sixteen to eighteen years. Here hormonal and sperm production is at peak capacity. At this stage of their development the urgent desire to engage in sex can be almost overwhelming. Physical attractions can really "send them." Not only does the sight (or touch) of the female form arouse them, but pictures, word pictures, and even thoughts have a similar effect. This no doubt is the basic reason why the "girlie" magazines are so popular. This supplies many males with much desired mental food for a built-in longing over which they have little control.

Once a male is aroused, and his internal motors are "turned on" there is often little hope of rebuffing him without causing a king-sized "scene." If he does not have some release to his pent-up emotions, he becomes frustrated, resentful, emotionally disturbed, and/or bad-tempered.

You have now told us the full story of going steady together with the possible pitfalls for the unwary and uninitiated.

What, then, is your advice for couples who wish to be sensible and stay out of harm's way as well as do what is socially acceptable as being right?

First, every young couple must be aware of the dangers that can overtake them when "going steady." Sensible ones will decide between themselves that sex and all that it entails (including pregnancy, rearing a family and the responsibilities attached to this delightful business) is for married life and definitely not before.

They will agree between themselves (maybe in words or by tacit, unmentioned but mutual agreement) that there will be no sex before wedding bells. They will then stick to this part of the deal, come what may, through thick and thin!

Is that all?

No, it is not. They will then act like two sensible human beings. In other words, they won't tempt fate (or nature, or call it what you like). They won't get themselves into compromising situations that are bound (with a reasonable degree of certainty) to lead on to sexual satisfaction. To be more specific, they will go places and enjoy themselves for sure. But sitting late at night in parked cars in dark alleyways, or in parking lots, or anywhere where they are remote and separate from the passing world, is not for them. Without a shadow of doubt, these are the places where moral danger lurks, unadulterated. This is where (the place and the time) your barriers are most likely to come down. This is when your built-in motors are going to get turned on. This is where you won't be able to stem the tremendous surging forces of nature. (Nature has you shackled at this point, remember.)

If your boyfriend suggests a clandestine cuddle in some quiet place, tell him to keep driving. Make specific times to be home and stick to the preplanned time schedule. After midnight time can fly by with lightning rapidity. The quicker it passes, the greater are the chances of your chastity being in peril—real peril.

Remember that your sex urges are naturally at a peak in midcycle. Also remember that this is the time when the possibility of pregnancy is at its height if sex is indulged in.

Keep well in mind the story of sex out of wedlock. The heartaches and mental anguish are definitely not worth the bit of fun that sex at this time can bring. In fact, many girls find sex the first few times a terrible disappointment. With the nervous tension and great emotional buildup, it often is an awful letdown. Invariably the male is the one who enjoys it most. Never forget this.

However, when it is all aboveboard, legal, and carried out within the bounds of marriage, it is completely different. Then it can be enjoyed with tenderness and desirability and the end point has no peer.

If your boyfriend commences vigorous petting, gently steer his wandering hands the other way. He'll soon get the message that certain parts of your anatomy are "out of bounds."

Although it may feel sensuous and quite enjoyable, do not let him touch your breasts or your thighs, and keep him clear of your very personal areas.

Just remember that although he makes the initial advances in most cases, once you commence to respond to his artful stimulation, very soon you will be engulfed by the great desire for which there is only one answer. Be firm. Even though your friend may fill your ears with all sorts of sweet nothings, tell you you're mean and cruel if you don't proceed with the lovemaking routine, be big enough to stand your ground firmly. Easy conquests are not appreciated by the average male. Just check, and 99 percent will tell you frankly (when pushed) they finally hope to marry a virgin!

How does that affect you? Girls of loose morals and easy virtue soon become well-known in male circles. Conquests are often chalked up and well discussed in male groups. How does that send you? Some of these points are well worth bearing in mind. They are not make-believe, and I am not talking through a hole in my neck. I hear these stories recounted with such regularity, and by girls from so many diverging walks of life, that I know they are true in every detail. Besides, my regular mail tells me what the spoken word cannot express.

This is a plea to young ladies everywhere for greater common sense before they get ensnared.

Chastity is an old-fashioned word. But have you noticed in recent years how old-fashioned things are coming back into unprecedented popularity again? I believe chastiy is on top of the list.

Don't you agree?

Lovely Skin and Fingernails

This title sounds like an interesting lineup.

I believe it affects a great number of teen-agers. In fact, I'm *sure* it does.

How can you be so positive?

I have only to rummage through the massive heap of letters I receive from young ladies throughout the nation to know how prevalent are these complaints. In fact, they arrive in their thousands, bagful after bagful.

Indeed, one magazine I regularly write for is beamed exclusively at teen-agers, and about half of the letters this column generates relate to skin, hair, nail, and weight problems! Therefore, I am absolutely *certain* young ladies build up enormous ideas in their minds of the importance of disorders in these areas.

Why do you think they are so important to them?

That's easy. You've only to look into a mirror yourself. What stares back at you? Nothing else but yourself! So many teen-agers spend so many hours a week peering at mirrors that it's virtually a national pastime.

Don't you think they'd be better off spending all these

precious hours doing something more constructive?

There is no doubt they would. But what's sensible and what's actually practiced are two entirely different things, remember?

It's simple for older people to sit and ponder over what youngsters *should* do; but it's a bit different if you're a teen-ager, and the problem is your own personal property. Every time you look into the mirror, a dozen nasty blackheads leap back at you. Every day, it seems, they increase in numbers, increase in size, and seem blacker, while the pimples seem redder, the skin more greasy, and the poor girl more uncomfortable and embarrassed. See what I mean?

Yes, I do. And I suppose the same problems occur with hair.

Very definitely. The hair won't grow fast enough. Or it grows *too* fast. Or it's curly, when the owner wants it to be straight. Or straight naturally, when wavy locks are the in thing.

Cracked, split ends are a continual annoyance. So is dull, lusterless hair. Falling hair is a nonstop problem, and the number of women who believe they'll be bald by the time they reach twenty-one is appalling.

Such a condition is a rarity, but the fear is present enough. Greasy scalps, dandruff, bald patches, facial hair, hairy arms and legs, and hair giving rise to "bikini problems" are all part of the seemingly never-ending list.

What about nails? Surely there can't be so many difficulties here.

No, fortunately. But lots of girls bite their fingernails. They want an easy "out" to cure this forever and "at once."

Others find that their nails break too easily. Of course many have problems that are related to sheer neglect of this important (and very obvious) part of the hands.

Pimples, Blackheads, Cysts, and Lumps

What aspect shall we discuss first?

I would like to delve into the skin problems. Seeing they are the commonest, they deserve position number one.

Shall we commence with the face? That is the part everyone looks at. It's also the area the mirror takes most notice of as well.

Sure. And pimples are the chief offender here. Acne vulgaris is the official title.

It can begin at any time after puberty. It seems to reach maximum intensity in the seventeen-to-eighteen-year age bracket. After this it tends to wane.

Thirty years of age is about the outside limit for women, although in males it can go on and cause problems even up to the age of forty or more!

You would say it's a self-limiting disease, then?

The tendency is for it to wane after the years of maximum activity. But this does not mean to say it should not be vigorously treated. Left unattended it can produce severe scarring. No girl appreciates unglamorous pockmarks even if there are no active pimples left.

What are the commonest parts affected?

The face (unluckily), shoulders, back, and chest are the key areas attacked. Therefore it is a disorder not confined solely to the exposed face.

Is there any particular pattern with the pimples?

Very definitely. The acne story revolves around pimples which we usually describe as blackheads. Technically these are called comedones. As they develop, they can turn into little superficial cysts. If you're unlucky, and germs climb aboard and infect these, they turn into more uncomfortable lumps called pustules. With the very unlucky these can penetrate more deeply. They then turn into painful abscesses. These are the ones that ultimately leave uneven scars.

What is the basic cause of acne?

During a time of development, as we've pointed out earlier, a sudden upsurge of hormones takes place internally. In male and female both male and female hormones are produced. However, more male hormones (called androgens) are produced in the male (giving rise to the secondary sex characteristics), while in the female a preponderance of female hormones (called estrogens) are manufactured. These cause the various attributes of the developing female form which we know so well.

Unfortunately, it's common in this riot of production for things to get a little out of hand. Often there occurs a hormonal imbalance. This means that there is a temporary irregularity or nonbalance of the proper hormonal components. Too much androgen in a girl's system can severely react on the skin surface and tiny sebaceous glands of the facial (and chest and back) skin layers.

The sebaceous glands are minute glands that occur in close proximity to the hair roots. They produce a chemical called sebum. This works its way out to the surface of the skin and forms a fine film over it. Basically it is designed to "waterproof" the skin. Otherwise we'd become waterlogged every time we went for a swim or took a bath! Imagine how disastrous that would be! Sometimes the sebaceous glands suddenly overproduce, and the little ducts or pipes taking the oily material to the surface become choked with the tremendous quantity they are trying to cope with.

So it jams up the works, and a pimple is born?

Exactly. The thing commences in a small way at first. But then it gradually swells up. Very soon chemical reactions take place with the whitish material inside, and it oxidizes and turns an unattractive black color. And so a blackhead is suddenly born.

What then?

It's really very simple. Like most things that start in a small way and are left to their own devices, they go from bad to worse. More sebum is produced and pumped into the pimple. It swells further. Then bacteria from the skin area tend to climb aboard. One very active germ called the acne bacillus is always ready and waiting to pounce into a blackhead and cause trouble.

Very soon a small sac full of debris and sebum forms. The blackhead has been developed into a cyst. A few more germs enter, and before long an infected cyst or pustule is present. If the pustule is not treated, the infection moves down the canal of the sebaceous gland and right into the gland itself.

At this stage, a most uncomfortable deep-seated cyst has really developed. These are painful, often causing considerable swelling and maybe a temperature; even touching them can evoke discomfort.

It strikes me that there is a little moral lesson to be learned from the acne story, don't you think?

I agree and have often pointed this out to patients. Like most things in this world, they commence in a small way. Maybe we can talk of habits (especially bad habits). They are tiny, microscopic, almost unnoticed at first. Attended to, they can often be removed at this point. But if they are left, they'll gradually grow, encompass a wider area, perhaps involve more people, become more firmly established, harder and gradually harder to eradicate. Ultimately, they are present in full force. They have become a major problem. To cure them also has become a marathon undertaking which is difficult, time-consuming and unattractive.

It matters little what the habit is; the procedure is identical.

It could be something simple (but foolish) like biting your fingernails. (This is a disgusting habit, to say the least, and really mars the beauty of many growing teenagers.) Or it could be something more sinister, such as the habit of smoking, indulging in social drinking, forming unsavory friendships. There is no limit.

If the situation is treated early, a cure is simple, reasonably effective, and often permanent. But left, it will gradually get the better of you. I feel that this is worth more than a passing mention.

What to Do for Acne

Now that we have the acne picture well in mind, comes the million-dollar question: What is the cure?

Million-dollar question? More likely it's fifty-million. I am certain untold sums of money are spent every year on useless "cures" for this perplexing, disfiguring problem, and all to no avail.

As a starter, my advice is to forget all the fancy well-advertised concoctions. In the initial stages at least, go for the simple ideas I'll outline here. They have stood the test of time over many years. True, they will not "cure" every case of acne. But they assist a great many and are worth a preliminary trial run.

Point number one?

Number one: Lots of soap and hot water are essential. Sounds simple, don't you agree? Yet according to my skin specialist colleague, "It's interesting that acne should begin so often in schoolgirls who as a class are well-known to have an aversion to soap and water!"

I prefer all pimply parts to be thoroughly washed. The idea is to remove the oily sebum that builds up on the skin surfaces.

Be most thorough on the areas affected most—the face, shoulders, back, and chest. On the face certain areas seem to suffer from oily build-up worse than other parts. The crevices between the nose and the cheeks, for example. There is the depression between the lower lip and the chin; the parts about the ears, and so on.

The heat and soap dissolve the oils, and the water flushes it all away, along with the germs that gather there. Some doctors suggest soaps and emulsions containing a germ-killer. This is often superior, but not essential.

What next?

Number two: Get rid of as many blackheads as possible. A comedo expresser may be used for this. This is a gadget shaped a bit like a small spoon with a hole in the center. The blackhead should first be wiped over with alcohol. The expresser is applied, gently rocked to and fro, and the black-head is expressed through the hole. It's essential to have an expresser with a small hole, preferably not greater than two millimeters in diameter. After this, a simple solution is placed over the area. (We'll detail this later.)

Some doctors find that gentle squeezing of the blackheads is quite satisfactory. After hot water washing, they often pop out with remarkable ease. If they do not, a hot pack for a short time will often have a similar successful effect. This should not be done persistently over long periods, and the pimples must not be clawed at with fingernails. Indeed, many young ladies stand in front of mirrors for hours firmly squeezing pimples with their nails. This can cause as much trouble as the original disorders! Pus-filled acne spots may be opened with a sterile needle. Infected, deep-seated ones may need the attention of a physician.

What is next in line after the blackheads have temporarily disappeared?

Number three: It's worth then applying a simple zinc-sulphur lotion. These abound in commercial prescription lines. However, one suggested a long time ago to me by my dermatology specialist has stood the test of time and still works in many cases. It can be made up at a pharmacy and consists of the following ingredients:

Zinc sulphate	4.5 parts
Pot. sulphurata	4 parts
Acetone	25 parts
Rose water to	100 parts

It is prepared as a lotion, applied by hand (not with cotton which absorbs too much of the fluid), and well rubbed into the skin until it has dried. Surplus powder will be rubbed off, though it is usually not obvious.

Seven to ten days later the skin may feel tight and rough. But it's essential to keep up the routine if we really want to obtain results.

Aren't there certain diet rules worth following with acne?

Definitely, and these come as point number four: Chocolate, and chocolate-containing foods are definitely out. Most experts agree on this one. It includes the entire range, from block chocolate to any sweets, cake, or drink containing chocolate. It definitely aggravates the disorder and must be considered taboo.

The experts aren't so certain about other foods. Some find the fatty foods aggravate acne. Others claim excess starches (potatoes, bread, cakes, sweets) will make it worse. So may nuts, spicy foods, and fried foods. You can see that more research is needed in this field.

What about general measures?

As point number five, these have a definite place. It's advisable to avoid emotional upsets. (How common these can be in this age segment!)

A sensible all-round general diet (high in protein and vitamins) is essential. Of course, this is also good for normal healthy living and vitality.

Most doctors prefer their patients to go off unnecessary medication. Many preparations can make acne worse, as some girls have found to their sorrow. Cosmetics and grease-based applications will further clog up pores and accentuate acne. Girls working in chemical plants with chemicals in the atmosphere can also run into problems.

Such factors as indigestion, constipation, and under-nourishment must be corrected promptly.

What if the condition persists despite all this good advice?

Then it is high time for the patient to visit the physician. He has lots of other gimmicks in his bag of tricks. For example, the tetracyclines, a family of "broad-spectrum antibiotics" often give excellent results when taken in low doses for prolonged periods.

The Pill seems to assist some girls. In others hormone therapy gives relief. Vitamin A is used in certain cases too.

What if scarring occurs?

Various measures help combat this. The antibiotics, the use of X rays by specialists, or the use of abrasive creams under proper supervision also assist. Once dermabrasion was used. Here the scar was "sandpapered" away. But it often caused redness, and infections sometimes occurred. Now this method is seldom used.

My advice to the thousands of girls who will read this is to follow the simple measures as suggested at the very beginning. This will often yield remarkably effective results if persisted with. A cursory effort for a day or two is hopeless. If there is no reasonable improvement after a few months, or if the condition is becoming worse, proper medical advice, of course, is essential.

Sunburn Hazards

In summer in many parts, sunbathing, swimming, surfing is the in thing for hot days. Sunburn, of course, is the perpetual trademark of this happy race of people. Or should I say "unhappy" race. What's your advice about sunburn?

I have very definite views. You see, of all skin disorders (and in fact of most disabilities in general) sunburn is an entirely preventable one. It should never occur. It comes merely because of carelessness and neglect.

It's easy to say this. Haven't you ever been to the beach?

I most certainly have. I simply love to surf. But every Monday morning in summer my office is crammed with suffering souls who have been indiscreet the previous day. And they want a magical cure to ease their burning epidermis and seared hides—plus several days off from school or work.

What is your reaction?

I do my best for them. But I can't help feeling how foolish each has been. Experience seldom yields results either. Year after year I see the same faces with the same complaint. "Will they never learn?" I ask myself. Seldom. Twenty years later I'm now seeing the children of the same people in the same sorry plight!

What is your recommendation, then?

Ideally, brown up well in advance of the burn-up season. This is my recipe for sun lovers and beach addicts.

Start four to six weeks before the summer surf season sets in. Get up a few minutes earlier every day. Lie in the early morning sun. Say for four minutes, front and back. Increase this by thirty to sixty seconds each morning. Within a remarkably short time you'll have the smartest tan around. Your friends will envy every square inch of your bronzed back!

Then by the time the first day of the official surfing season arrives, you'll have automatically donned the best armor protection available.

Supposing one has forgotten or didn't have time (or the inclination)?

Then take it *easy* on the first trip to the beach. Do *not* overexpose. Take only a few short dives in the water. When you come out, make absolutely certain your exposed parts are well protected.

Don't think you'll escape burning merely because you sit under a big beach umbrella. Disastrous heat rays bounce back from any light-colored expanse. This includes sheets of water, expanses of sand, masses of fleecy white clouds. All are expert reflectors. It's made worse if there is a dry wind blowing.

(Also, don't forget large expanses of snow if you happen to be a skier. Sunburn hazards here are likewise enormous.)

Put a lightweight covering over your body. Don't forget arms and legs and also the feet. They are terribly painful when burned.

Are the sunburn creams any good?

The only ones that are worth buying are those containing an active ultraviolet light filter. Many do, but again lots do not. Ask your doctor for a reliable brand name, and stick with this.

Don't forget, most of these are water-soluble. Therefore, they must be reapplied often throughout the day—including each time you come from the water. But do not rely on them too heavily. Use them in conjunction with common sense and suitable protective covering.

What if all this valuable advice has been ignored and a harsh burning has been acquired?

Get home promptly. Often a good hot soak or shower will take the immediate sting out of the burn. In severe cases, and particularly if blistering has occurred, frequent applications of cold water are best. Do not burst blisters, for this will allow germs to gain entry, and infections can result. This way you'll be worse off than ever.

Lots of fluid intake is essential. Sometimes a pinch of salt added to this helps replace the loss of important "electrolytes" from the system. I like to give frequent chilled fruit juices to which powdered glucose D has been added (one teaspoon per glass of fluid). Repeat often.

Paracetamol tablets are often effective if the pain is severe. Don't be duped into purchasing expensive "sunburn cure creams." These are usually only transient in their effect, contain local anesthetics which sometimes cause rashes, and can leave you worse off than ever. The sum spent annually by gullible people is astronomical when it comes to sunburn cures. Prevention in the first instance is the only cure, and this is what we recommend.

Warts

Do you find many young ladies are troubled with warts?

Yes, it's a common disorder. It's believed they're caused by a minute virus. This gets into the upper skin layers and causes the skin there to grow rapidly. As it has nowhere else to go, it simply heaps up in the form of an unattractive lump. So a wart is born. The clinicians refer to them as Verruca vulgaris. It sounds nicer than old *warts!*

Is there a simple way to get rid of them?

You'd be amazed at the range of weird home cures that have proved successful over the years. Like milk thistle fluid, and rubbing them with a penny, or "selling them to the milkman," or wrapping them up for twenty-four hours with the inside of a banana skin next to the wart! You name it, someone has tried it. And been cured!

How come? I thought hocus pocus went out with the Dark Ages!

I agree. But autohypnosis (or call it what you like)—some call it psychotherapy—continues to get rid of lots of warts.

The skin is closely tied up with the nervous system. Apparently, if you believe something firmly enough, it can unconsciously "cure" you. This is very common in the case of warts.

Lots of simple chemical cures are often successful. A simple one is podophyllin, 20 percent in friar's balsam. This is dabbed on the wart (not the surrounding skin) with the end of a match or toothpick each night. It's believed it stops the cells multiplying, and bit by bit the lump regresses and finally disappears.

Glacial acetic acid is used in a similar way. But be very careful not to upset the bottle or get the acid near the eyes. It is very potent.

A doctor's simple prescription is this:

> Salicylic acid   3.6
> Alcohol 40 percent   q.s. ad 120
> Apply to the warts with a cotton swab
> stick each night.

Your druggist could readily prepare this for you.

What if these fail to cure?

At this stage it's wise to visit the doctor. A favorite method is for him to remove the wart with a scalpel or small curette under local anesthetic. The wound is then diathermied lightly. It can take up to a couple of weeks to heal across. Under no circumstances try to remove the wart by yourself. Warts have a habit of bleeding profusely, and this can be difficult to stop unaided.

Do not fiddle past the simple measures suggested above. If a wart is knocked, it can also bleed ferociously. Wrap firmly and get to the doctor who will complete the job of removing it and sealing off bleeding points.

You told me recently you often had requests for the removal of scars and tattoo marks, of all things.

Yes. Every week someone writes and tells me of a past love affair. Either the girl (but more commonly the boy) has had the name of her/his friend tattooed on some prominent part. The backs of the fingers are a common spot! The upper outer part of the arm is also popular, and so is the chest.

The embarrassing situation is when "Jane" is displayed prominently for all the world to see. And now Jane has been phased out of the picture, and "Cynthia" is the current favorite! Cynthia doesn't take too kindly to the persistent reminder of Jane before her eyes every time she meets her boyfriend.

How can the name be erased forever?

This is usually a job for the plastic surgeons. They are experts at erasing names of girls (or boys) that are no longer current. I often wonder how many romances they patch up with their scalpels and thread.

Scars can also be removed this way. These are common following motor vehicle accidents where broken glass has set up multitudes of skin blemishes.

The results are often incredibly good. Your own family doctor will direct you to the right consultant for this sort of work. I advise "no fiddling." You can only aggravate and often make it worse. However, certain masking cosmetics can give temporary respite and are certainly worth a trial run.

"Cold Sores"

What do you think about cold sores?

Cold sores, of course, have nothing to do with colds! These little blisters that accumulate around the lips, under the nostrils, about the chin, and even on the cheeks are virus-induced. Often the glands under the chin become swollen and very sore as well.

What is a simple cure?

There is no universal cure. Simply dabbing the blisters frequently with a patented preparation such as Blistex is often effective. Apply often. Try to avoid the precipitating factors. Avoid exposure to hot sun, especially early in the season when you are not accustomed to harsh ultraviolet rays.

Keep free from allergies. (Many young people know what they're allergic to. Avoid these foods, cosmetics, or whatever as much as possible.)

Nervous system upsets and domestic squabbles are notorious for bringing these sores on. Boyfriend disagreements possibly head the list. A bunch of blisters about the lips does nothing to calm the spirits the day following a squabble. Neither does it improve the looks or increase your desirability in the eyes of the boyfriend!

What about persistent cases?

These need proper medical attention. Sometimes the physicians give a series of smallpox vaccinations. These often work efficiently in checking further outbreaks.

A recently developed drug (now commercially available) is claimed to kill the virus, provided it's applied in the very early stages before the appearance of the blisters. This can be obtained and used only under medical supervision however.

I think the main thing is to know that these preparations are available. It's then up to your own doctor.

Hives and Skin Blotches

Don't lots of teen-agers get hives?

Yes, lots of them suffer from these horrid red, itchy, hot, irritating swellings.

I believe they are allergy-induced also?

That's quite true. The system has become sensitized to a certain product (usually a protein). After this, whenever the protein is again contacted, a potent chemical called histamine is liberated by the system.

This chemical races around (via the bloodstream) to all parts of the body. It can initiate all manner of symptoms.

For example, hives are the skin component of the reaction. But it starts "hay fever" as well. (I'm sure you've seen your hay-fever friends sniffling and sneezing when the pollens are floating around in space, midspring to summer.) Severe instances can even produce asthma in susceptible patients.

What can be done about the hives?

Symptomatically, the local application of an antipruritic cream is the simplest and most relieving. This is a simple cream containing various ingredients that are known for their power to combat itching and irritation. (For example benzocaine, menthol, tar.) There are many creams readily available for this purpose. Most are quite effective. Use for the minimum amount of time which gives results.

But isn't this basically all wrong? Shouldn't the patient be looking for the cause of the problem if it's due to a foreign protein, as you say?

By all means. But it is not so simple to track this down. It may be something quite obvious. Often some people are very sensitive to certain foods. Sea foods are notorious for causing allergies. Especially the crustacean family—lobster, prawns, and that class of food. Lots of berries are similarly problematical: strawberries and the like.

Maybe it's something that has been contacted rather than eaten. New clothing is well known. So are soaps, detergents, cosmetics. However, many cases are transitory, and the simple creams will settle them down. More protracted ones need the antihistamine tablets for a day or two. (These neutralize the effect of the system's histamine and so bring relief.)

More severe cases that keep on keeping on may need the final assistance of the allergy specialist. He will ferret out the troublemaker. In some cases, desensitization injections are needed for final cure.

Fingernail Beauty

How can a girl achieve lovely fingernails?

I'm glad you asked me this. So many young ladies have beautiful nails. But others have the most horrible ones imaginable.

You know, fingernail care is very important. It's essential to correct grooming. I feel that a person doesn't look completely dressed unless the nails are properly cared for. It is so obvious if care is lacking here.

What is some good general advice? I'm sure all our readers would prefer to have attractive nails.

Regular cleansing is essential. What's better than a not-too-hard nail brush plus lots of warm water and soap? Not only does this remove the dirt from underneath, but it assists circulation in the fingertips, and this in turn makes sure the nails have a nice, healthy bed from which to grow.

You know the nail is a dead structure. It grows from the *nail bed* which is located just beneath the skin a short distance below the base of the nail itself where it protrudes from the skin margin. Any dirt that remains must be removed with a suitable instrument. It is desirable to keep the cuticle pushed well back. This will expose the lovely half-moons which are characteristic of carefully manicured nails.

Do you condone nail files?

Personally I do not like metal files. (I know that millions

use them, but better results are available using other methods.) Nails should be kept at a reasonable length. Use nail scissors once a week (or two, depending on rate of growth). Then file them smooth with emery boards rather than metal files. File inward to the center of the nail. Make certain all jagged edges are smoothed away.

What do you think about polishes and paints for the nails?

It's really a matter of personal choice. However, quite a lot of damage to the nails can occur with varnishes and cuticle removers. These often contain harsh caustics. They can make the nails brittle with a tendency to break easily. Girls hate their nails always cracking and breaking off.

I was coming to this. What really causes nail brittleness and the tendency to break–apart from the reason you have mentioned?

There are many known reasons. Even mild degrees of ill health can reflect back into the nails and make them brittle. Mild anemias (inadequate iron in the system causing poor quality blood) are another well-established cause. This responds well to simple oral iron preparations.

I favor the oral administration of calcium also for weak nails. It seems to help. (Drink more milk if you're having problems. This is the simplest way to take more calcium aboard each day.) Some people claim gelatin each day helps too, but I personally have my doubts about this.

Following illnesses, the too frequent use of excessive soap, nail varnishes, removers, and alkaline cleaners will aggravate the situation.

Any persisting nail problem should have the attention of your own doctor if simple measures do not fix the trouble fairly quickly.

What about the nail biters?

I'd like to make special reference to this problem. It is so widespread, and it can be most humiliating. Invariably it's the tense, nervous person who chews the fingernails in moments of mental tension.

"It took me four solid months to grow my nails—plus persistence and much self-control. Then I watched a tense, action-packed TV show one night. And in five minutes flat my ten nails had gone. Disaster! I just didn't know I was chewing them to pieces." So ran the self-confession of an attractive eighteen year old who had tried desperately to stem the habit.

Do you have a cure?

I firmly believe it's like any habit. Once established (and this usually occurs in early childhood) it is terribly hard to break.

Self-control and sheer determination are the main bulkheads of success. So is positive thinking. Telling yourself you will lick the habit is essential. You must *convince* yourself. Then the rest is not so difficult. It's largely up to you and how much you really want to relinquish the habit. However, just to make it a bit more easy, I *do* have a little system that can assist no end. In fact, I've suggested it to many teen-agers over the years, and the majority claim it works.

It involves the wearing for about three months of false fingernails. If these are applied for some time, the proper nail grows up inside the false one. You won't bite the false one—it just doesn't seem natural.

By the time the natural one has grown up, you've more or less got out of the way of nibbling; so the habit tends to wane.

However, don't be fooled. Go easy on your TV fare. Beware of circumstances when tensions run riot, these are the occasions when you're very likely to have a king-sized nibble once more. Then it's "Disaster Unlimited" again!

II

All About Hair Care

Do you mind if we come on the the very important question of hair? Right at the start you said you receive thousands of queries on this vital topic.

How true. In fact, so popular is the question that, on the average, I'd say I produce a story regularly every other week on hair care and hair problems! Hair difficulties generate an enormous number of letters from youngsters all over the nation.

Why do you think this is so?

I'm certain hair forms a very important part of the body. It is obvious, to say the least. "It's a glory to her," Paul said. Indeed, I suppose more time and effort is expended on this particular area than on any other single part of the anatomy.

But isn't hair really "dead"?

To be sure it is. (But please don't quote me. Women would *hate* to think of their hair as something that's lifeless!)

The hair actually comes from a growing point called the bulb. This is deeply located in the lower layers of the skin of the scalp. It is nourished by copious blood vessels. It pushes its way through the upper layers to the surface. As long as the bulb remains alive and healthy, new hair is being constantly produced.

Once the hair strand leaves the bulb it no longer grows. It is like the fingernail once it has left the growing point which is the nail bed. So, in effect, hair is not a viable organ once it has left the point of production.

Its basic purpose is quite simple. It protects the vital organs located in the cranial vault—the brain and the key nervous networks. It protects them from temperature variations, and can also play a part in cushioning direct trauma.

So, for no other purpose than this, the hair is vitally important, especially so in hot climates, and where the individual may be exposed to the elements. Do not consider your hair merely as an item of beauty. Picture it in the overall concept as being a useful and indeed essential part of your system, just like your arms and legs, only in a different sense.

Isn't the hair strand connected to the sebaceous glands somehow?

Yes. Before it surfaces, a small gland (or maybe several of them) called the sebaceous gland, runs in close proximity to the hair shaft. In fact, they may surface together.

The sebaceous gland, as we pointed out earlier, produces an oily material that waterproofs the skin. However, the sebum (as the material is called) also tends to cover the hair shaft as well.

Now please bear this well in mind, for certain scalp-hair problems are intimately associated with this fact.

The Commonest Problem

What would you say would be the commonest problem of the hair and scalp?

The one that troubles people from all parts of the world on a never-ending basis is the simple, horrible scourge known as dandruff. It causes irritation, discomfort, and even dismay everywhere.

Isn't that the condition which produces a mass of tiny, white, confettilike scales that fly in all directions whenever the hair is disturbed?

Yes, it's called all sorts of names. (Many are rude, a few are polite, some are technical.)

Dandruff, scurf, pityriasis capitis, and seborrhea sicca are all synonyms for dandruff.

What causes this?

It's a combination of various factors. Basically, they are flakes of the outer horny layer of the skin, plus partially dried-out sebum. In fact, the scalp has become infected with a minute germ called the pityrosporon. This has caused the scalp layers to react and so produce the excess cells which finally flake off when disturbed. The scales are usually white, but if a lot of sebum is mixed with them, they turn a yellow color and appear greasy.

Are dandruff flakes infectious?

Very infectious. The scales are packed with the dandruff germs. In fact, babies are often infected by scales dropping on them from their mother or nurse. It's very easy for one person to infect another, especially when combs and brushes are used in hairdressing solons where the sterilizing systems are frequently not all they could be.

What's the chief concern with dandruff?

The outcome can be disastrous, to say the least. It can cause premature death of the hair bulb. Once dead, it's gone forever. The bulb does not regenerate again. It doesn't matter what your (or any) hairdresser tells you, once dead, the hair bulb is dead. Forever.

Also, dandruff can predispose to a conditon called seborrheic dermatitis. This is a horrid disorder of the sebaceous glands. Excessive amounts of sebum are produced. It forms an unattractive, irritating, weeping mess that looks a fright and causes pronounced discomfort.

Once more we come to the big question of the moment. What is the best way to treat dandruff?

Fortunately, a couple of very satisfactory preparations are now widely available which bring dandruff under quick control. One is called selenium sulphide, and it comes in a shampoo form. (There are various commerical varieties of this. This is the chemical name of the preparation.)

Usually, the shampoo is used twice weekly to start with, and after the initial burst, as often as necessary to keep the scalp free from itching and scaling. Generally, enough shampoo is applied to wet the scalp and form a lather. Work it thoroughly into the hair and scalp. Let it remain on for two or three minutes; then rinse thoroughly. This procedure may be repeated several times. It's advisable to keep this away from the eyes. The full directions usually come with the product.

What's the other one you mentioned?

A more recent product is the chemical called zinc pyridinethione or zinc pyrithione. They are similar. A small amount is applied and worked into a good lather. This is washed off and the procedure repeated. Once the dandruff is cleared, the preparation is used again from time to time to prevent recurrences.

This is also available as a hair cream dressing, but this is more suitable for males with recurring dandruff problems. It is extremely effective and is used widely.

What about general measures. Is there anything here worth advising?

Certainly. General attention to commonsense health principles is important. It plays a part. Having a well-balanced, nourishing diet is important. Regular working hours, atten-

tion to getting eight hours' sleep a night, simple, general
cleanliness, avoiding constipation, avoiding alcohol and excessive amounts of spicy fare and hot drinks are believed to
play a part. Just how much, we are not certain. But if the
scalp disorders are your problem in life, it's worth following
all available ideas in an effort to get rid of them.

Split Hairs

*What's good for broken hairs and hairs with split ends?
This seems a very common teen-age problem.*

First let's have a closer look at the hair shaft itself. This
consists of an inner part called the medulla and an outer part
termed the cortex. Lying on the cortex are very fine, microscopic scales.

Now, once the hair is broken at the far end, it will very
easily crack along its length. In fact, it can crack right down
the medulla and extend for a long way. This gives the hair
ends an unattractive appearance. Indeed, many, many girls
have this as a giant-sized personal complaint.

Is there a cure for this?

The only cure is to cut off the broken split ends. They
cannot possibly regenerate from the outside end. The cracks
will only grow worse.

The common cause for this problem is excessive combing
with combs in which the teeth are too short and set too
closely together. Also, rough handling of the hair is another
notorious cause.

Hair is very vulnerable to severe handling. It must be
treated kindly and gently. I keep telling my young friends
this, but I'm afraid the information more often than not falls
on deaf ears.

Teasing the hair is about the best way yet devised to
destroy its attractive appearance. This enjoys passing popu-

larity from time to time. It is disastrous on hair.

To avoid this it is essential to use a comb with long teeth. The teeth should be set at fairly wide intervals.

Of course, the best way to treat the hair is to *brush* it regularly. Use a bristle brush. Pig bristles are the best. They are far superior to plastic and synthetic bristles. If you have the choice, go for pig bristles. It's well worth the additional cost.

Falling Hair; Lusterless Hair

Lots of girls complain that their hair falls out. What's the cause of this?

Quite often this too is self-inflicted. Wearing hair in rollers that are too tight is often the cause. This can exert a tremendous, continual pull on the hair bulb. Often the hair merely gives up the fight and loosens from its moorings. Presto! Out it drops!

I'd say this is about the commonest cause for falling hair. So if this is *your* hair problem, revise your methods at once. (Tonight, as a start.) Completely review your hairdressing habits, and maybe your problems will ease very rapidly.

What's the cause of dull, lusterless hair? According to my newspaper gleanings, this is due to "lack of this, lack of that," "try Brand X" "massage in Brand Y and you'll be cured. Forever!" Is this true, or a lot of hocus pocus?

The national bill rung up on hair care products would boggle the imagination. What's more, it is increasing sharply every year. It's a wonderful game for the advertising people. Women are wonderful when it comes to spending fortunes on magical remedies (so-called) that will make their locks sparkle as never before. Forget them all!

In fact, a tremendous number of products claimed to improve the hair actually have the opposite effect. It worsens what it's supposed to improve! There is no doubt about this. Ask any hair-care expert, and it will be readily confirmed.

Almost any chemical applied to the hair will reduce its sheen. There are thousands of hair sprays, dyes, bleaches, rinses. These universally tend to remove the microscopic layer of sebum which naturally covers the hair shaft. It's the sebum that gives the hair its characteristic healthy sparkle. Remove it, and the hair becomes dead, lusterless, lacking in vitality.

I am certain that 90 percent of women have no idea of the power of the chemicals they slap on their hair with gay abandon. Most are very strong and can literally wreck lovely hair.

I am afraid some hairdressers (especially the backyard-business ones) are not familiar with the sting of the material they hand out to their customers.

How can all this be avoided then?

It's imperative that you attend only qualified, registered hairdressers. This at least gives you some guarantee of protection. A properly trained, qualified, and registered person has been through a proper course of instruction. Such a person has learned the basics of good hairdressing, knows what is involved, and appreciates the power of the materials being used. A trained hairdresser has passed an examination (or indeed, no doubt, a series of exams over a period of several years' training).

To qualify for registration, anyone must have become properly qualified and demonstrated efficiency as a guardian of human hair. It's well worth bearing this in mind, particularly if you are already experiencing hair problems.

It's also worth reviewing your own actions if you're a home "do-it-yourself" enthusiast. It just may be possible that you are doing yourself more harm (in all innocence) tampering

with products about which you know very little.

It's worth more than passing consideration. This is not a plug for the hairdressing profession either. It's just sensible advice gleaned from many years' firsthand experience with those who have suffered most—the long-suffering (but often self-inflicted) members of the public! They go like lambs to the slaughter.

Are there other causes of lusterless hair that should be mentioned?

Yes. Many people are oblivious to the rigors of the elements when it comes to their hair. The sun, wind, rain, salt air, surf, and/or chemicals in swimming pools can all play a part in tearing hair to pieces.

When out of doors, and especially when the elements are severe, you should see that your hair is covered. (Ever noticed how the Europeans and Orientals do this even when they're transplanted to other lands?)

After surfing or a swim, rinse the hair thoroughly and remove all traces of salt and other chemicals that might be present.

Washing and Brushing

How often should the hair be washed?

The hair should be washed at least once a week. If it is oily, this must be done every second or third night. Otherwise, there will be a buildup of sebum and the tendency to dandruff formation. The dandruff germ is quick to attack when scales are present.

Should soaps or shampoos be used?

A soapless, detergent-based shampoo is by far the best. Soaps are full of chemicals and are harsh and tend to leave a fine film on the hair shaft. Shampoos will not do this. They quickly remove dirt and tend to leave a sheen.

Do you go along with the "100 brushes a night" deal?

I certainly go for lots of brushing of the hair. It needn't be exactly 100 times, but the more the better, and the more often this is done, the better, as well.

What does it do?

Brushing makes the sebum layer on the shaft sparkle. It also smooths the fine scales on the cortex and places them in a position where they tend to reflect light and also add to the vital sheen that every girl loves.

Besides brushing, massaging the scalp is very good. This helps blood circulation in the scalp. It brings fresh blood to the hair bulb and keeps it in a vital, healthy state of growth.

Slow-growing Hair

What do you tell girls who complain that their hair grows too slowly? You showed me several letters from girls who claimed their hair grew to a certain length and stayed there indefinitely.

I am afraid this is sheer imagination on their part. The longer the hair becomes, of course, the progressively longer it *seems* to be taking to increase further. It's all relative.

Whiskers on a male face are there every morning. But just let a male try and grow a beard, and it seems to take ages! It is all relative.

Hair grows half an inch per month—fast enough for anyone.

So if your hair seems to have come to a sudden halt, it really has not. Do not despair. It will continue at this rate irrespective of what you do. However, attention to hygiene, massaging of the scalp and the brushing routine we've mentioned earlier will certainly assist. It won't make the hair grow any more rapidly. But it will ensure that the hair is kept healthy and that it will maintain its steady growth rate.

Unwanted Hair

Some girls are really worried about hair growing in abnormal places. What are your views on this?

This is certainly a universal problem shared by millions of girls and older women everywhere.

The chief areas of concern are: (1) the face, (2) the arms, (3) the legs, and (4) the pubic areas.

What's the advice for this suffering army?

It depends a lot on the degree to which the problem is a problem.

In broad terms, obvious facial hairs are dealt with this way: The depilatory creams are excellent for immediate (but not lasting) results.

There are many excellent commerical brands available. The cream is applied. It's left there for a few minutes and then removed. The hair cracks off at the skin surface. However, like whiskers on a man's face, they soon reappear. The cream must be reapplied whenever the hair stumps become obvious again.

Is there a permanent cure?

Yes. Electrolysis is the best cure for all time. Here an operator skilled in the art extends an electric needle down the hair shaft to the bulb. The current is turned on momentarily, and the hair root is permanently destroyed. It will not regenerate.

My advice for anyone seeking this is to find an expert. If done by poorly trained operators, too much current may be applied. This can have the effect of leaving a minute scar at the site where the hair shaft extends from the skin margin. However, the experts' services are reasonably priced and give excellent results.

Hairs above the upper lip are a common source of annoyance. These can effectively be removed this way at a price not beyond the economics of most girls.

What about the bleaches?

This is sometimes adequate in girls with dark facial hair. However, the other systems are more popular in general.

What about hairs on the arms and legs?

Often these areas are too vast for electrolysis to be a proposition. It would be too costly and take too long. Therefore the depilatory creams (or lotions) are often used. With the legs, depilatory waxes are popular. (This is not suitable for the face, for it tends to remove the soft feminine "down" as well.)

The wax comes in kits. It is heated, placed on the affected area, and allowed to cool. Then it is quickly removed. Hairs (bulbs and all) come away. Some claim it permanently removes the problems, others find that it has to be redone many times over for good results. Some find the use of pumice abrasive on the legs satisfactory.

What about shaving with a razor?

I am against this, for I feel it gives an unsatisfactory general result. I also think it has to be done too often to be really effective, and this in time can make the skin coarse and tough, much like a male face with years of persistent shaving.

You mentioned something about "bikini problems" with many young people in summer months. What's this all about?

For some unknown reason, Western women equate hair (other than on the scalp) with a lack of femininity. Therefore, it is frowned upon, and every effort is expended to get rid of it.

However, hair grows in certain anatomical parts despite what fashion (and mental attitudes) decree. The pubic area is one of these. (Under the arms is another, but we'll deal with that later on.)

It's just part of nature's design. It's most likely a built-in modesty factor. However, with the increasing popularity of beach wear, lots of girls discover to their dismay that hair in this particular area tends to peep from underneath. Or with others, the growth extends down farther than average. Disaster! We are forever being asked how this may be overcome.

What is the answer to the problem?

My usual ready answer is the obvious one. If the gear they're wearing is so revealing, then it's probably high time for reassessing (and redesigning) their beach apparel.

However, where hair growth is definitely greater than normal, any of the methods already mentioned can be used here too.

Because of the fairly brief nature of summer months, the depilatory lotions are perhaps the simplest and quickest and cheapest answer to the problem. If a more "forever" cure is desired, electrolysis again is the answer.

What about underarm hair?

The same routines are available. The depilatory lotions are perhaps the most widely used and safest. I'm dead against shaving with razors. I've seen too many cases of severe infections in the armpit to view the method with equanimity. It is so easy to make a minor nick. Very quickly germs can gain an entrance and establish nasty infections, especially in the axillary lymph glands which are numerous in this region. I think I prefer the lotions. Electrolysis and waxes are hardly suitable for this area.

Other Hair Blemishes

Are there any other hair problems worth mentioning?

Yes, there are a couple of recurring ones that cause widespread torment to young women. These are hairs on the breasts! Once more these are mentally related to the typical hairiness of the male chest and are considered "not feminine." It is very common and in fact can hardly be regarded as abnormal.

Often the problem is one single long hair somewhere near the nipple. Or it might be half a dozen that keep growing, despite regular clipping. Less commonly, many hairs grow from the general breast region.

What is your advice?

I believe the permanent removal of the hairs by electrolysis is the quickest and most satisfactory cure in this region. It's painless and effective and does much to reestablish mental peace and calm.

What is the other "at risk" spot?

Moles and facial blemishes that sprout hairs.

What is the best line of treatment in these parts?

Personally, I'm not keen on these being fiddled with until a skilled physician has examined the part.

Dark moles, in particular, should be treated with great caution. Many of these are the precursor to the most dangerous form of cancer known. Malignant melanoma is the technical name we use.

Fiddling with these in their early stages can be fraught with potential disaster. If there is any doubt as to their nature, the surgeon will have the part properly removed and examined. Never let a nonprofessional person tamper with moles anywhere on your anatomy.

Do you really mean that these innocuous-looking moles can be disastrous?

I certainly do! Malignant cells from these areas have an uncanny ability of racing madly to all parts of the body. Within an incredibly short time they can kill. Swiftly, silently, with deadly accuracy. In fact, any black or dark-blue mole anywhere must be examined at first detection by a doctor. Never neglect them. *Never!*

What about some of the other commonly occurring skin "blemishes" so often seen, especially in the hot climates?

Any flaking sore must be regarded with suspicion. In tropical and subtropical climates skin cancers are very common.

They often start as tiny, red marks. A flake occurs, comes away, re-forms. Six months later, it's still going on in this way. But underneath, silently, a minute skin cancer is forming. Gradually it enlarges, spreads, and eventually develops into a full-blown cancer.

Fortunately, because they're usually obvious, most people have the sense to get medical attention at a reasonable stage. But it is incredible in these days of universal knowledge on the hazards of cancer how many will prod and poke at these things on a regular daily basis, year in year out.

In fact, a fellow who visited my place regularly (he was one of the tradesmen) gradually developed a cancer on his ear. Purely as a gesture of goodwill, I pointed this out to him one day. Action, I urged, was imperative. He said he'd think about it. Six months later he visited me officially, and suggested I do something. By this time, the cancer had grown to twice the size.

I arranged for him to see my skin specialist colleague. A time was made. But the tradesman, whom we'll call Bob, was too busy to keep the appointment. Bob's ear lesion gradually smoldered on, becoming bigger as the months ticked by. I rarely saw him as I was busy too, and didn't have cause to hunt him out to check on progress. (After all it was *his* ear, his life.)

Bob finally managed to see the skin expert. He was horrified. The cancer was larger than ever, of course. Just the same, surgery was arranged. Before Bob could escape this time (for the nth time), further arrangements were made for the hospital, and the fellow was pinned down to a firm commitment.

But just as in times past, he again eluded us all. He failed to arrive at the hospital at the appointed time.

A few months later, he again turned up. This time he was really worried himself, a situation rare for the nonchalant Bob. "Must be fixed this time," he emphatically promised.

Within a day the sinister cancer had been removed. But now it was deep, disastrous. Most of his ear and much of the surrounding area had to be removed. Before he left the hospital, a routine chest X ray was taken, just to make certain nothing was occurring deep down. Bob escaped before the films were ready for inspection.

But by this time, it probably didn't matter much. The X rays told their own story. The cancer had spread to the lungs. Now it was merely a matter of time!

Although we tried to contact our elusive patient, he was simply not available.

We haven't seen him since and aren't likely to. He's either passed on forever or is still living out a miserable final sojourn before being collected by the grim reaper. And all over a simple lesion that could have been easily removed had he given us the opportunity at the time he was first seen.

If you have some obvious lesion in some place, do not be guilty of the stupidity of Bob. *Get medical attention at once.*

It could save you endless hours of misery; not necessarily now, but at the other end of the line when it matters most.

This true story of Bob, despite today's widespread anticancer publicity, is being repeated over and over. It's amazing, but true. Like the ostriches who are supposed to bury their heads in sand, some people are too foolish to face up to the realities of life. They prefer to neglect themselves. But they pay the price ultimately—without fail.

Bosom Beauty

How important are "figure problems" with teen-age girls?

I'm glad you've come around to this very important topic. I believe the average teen-ager spends a tremendous amount of time worrying about her "figure." In fact, problems along these lines would be the number one contender, judging by the countless thousands of letters I regularly receive.

Is it simply a matter of weight that upsets the majority?

It's either weight or a lack of it. But another important aspect is the distribution of this weight.

The common problems involve general overweight, with an emphasis on fat stomachs, unsightly hips and buttocks, thick "unfeminine" legs and arms.

What about "bosom beauty"?

These days, everybody—but everybody, it seems—worships the female bosom. The advertising people are to blame for this to a large extent. However, I'm afraid clinicians are a little more down to earth and regard the female breast for what it really is: a source of food for the next generation in its infancy.

But these overzealous advertising men have converted it

into something more than this. They've developed a real hang-up about it. It's the in thing for all women to have chest measurements within certain accepted norms.

Does this have any serious consequences?

It most certainly does. Millions of young women believe they are "abnormal" simply because their bosom development is either less (or more uncommonly, greater) than what's become accepted as the "ideal."

The really disastrous moment comes when they take this to heart. And tremendous numbers of young women do just this. They develop a psychological phobia about their appearance. Many believe they are inferior to their peers simply because of this structural deviation.

I receive letters by the score from girls who believe their lives are being destroyed because nature hasn't been kind to them!

What They Say

What are their comments, for example?

There are many ways of expressing the same thing. For instance: "My chest is as flat as a board. I look simply terrible in a bathing suit. None of the fellows gives me a second look."

Or: "My bosom development is far below normal. My clothes just hang and look hideous. Can I have an operation to fix my problem?"

Or: "Nature hasn't been very kind to me. Now I've got a king-sized inferiority complex. It's all I can think about day after day. How can I improve my chest dimensions?"

On and on they go, all variations of the same strange complaint.

Usually lack of chest development (as they call it) is equated with failure in life and with the inability to be attractive to the male segment of the species.

Others, it seems spend so much time gazing at their bodies in the mirror and worrying themselves sick that in fact they *do* become sick—sick in mind, if not in body.

This rebounds on them and makes them less attentive at school. So they tend to make poorer grades. All this in turn gives them a feeling of inferiority, of being of lesser importance (physically and mentally) than other girls who are better endowed by nature.

What is your advice to these unhappy girls?

First I point out one very important fact. This is the basic nature and function of the bosom. It's been produced solely to feed the prospective mother's infant. All females are potential mothers.

From experience we know it matters not one jot what the size of the bosom is in this respect. Small bosoms are often the best milk producers when the time comes.

I've proved this time and again with my obstetric patients. I tell this to my prospective mothers-to-be if they start complaining of their small breast size in early pregnancy.

Conversely, women with apparently well-developed and shapely breasts often are deficient in this department, many of them running into significant feeding difficulties later on. Indeed, many have to wean their babies early. In fact, some find it quite impossible to breast-feed at all!

I hope this does a great deal to encourage and lighten the mental load of the small-chested women.

Bosom Development

That is very enlightening information. But in the teens the majority of women are not contemplating breast-feeding babies in the very near future. "Now" is the time they're concerned about. Is there any universally successful way in which bosom development can be encouraged or improved upon?

The answer to this, of course, is No! I know there are masses of advertisements promising this and that. But they are all frauds. No single means exists of adding inches to undersized chests.

But surely there must be some methods worth trying!

Most certainly. I believe a sensible approach to food is essential. A high protein, high vitamin intake, and a reasonable carbohydrate intake, are necessary for general good health.

If the general system is in good tone, then the chest must reflect this as well.

Next, exercises play a part. By developing the major chest muscles, what is present in the way of breast tissue will be given as much prominence as possible. Any of the vigorous outdoor sports are good, particularly those utilizing the upper limbs. Swimming is ideal. So is surfing and any other water sport. Here the arms are being used to the maximum.

Other sports such as tennis and basketball are good as well. Gymnastics and any exercise routine that involves use of the upper limb and chest muscles must play a part in increasing development and tone of the big pectoral muscles that form the front part of the chest.

Outdoor exercise keeps the system in good tone, the muscles generally free from excess fat and flab. Not only will the chest muscles benefit, but the entire body must be better off. Experience definitely proves the worth of this.

The Pill and Injections

What about the Pill? We often hear that this improves the figure.

As a means of giving permanent improvement to the chest

dimensions it is definitely out. The Pill, so widely used for family planning, is a combination of two potent hormones. In fact, when ingested, it gives a chemical state inside the body similar to that existing in the early months of pregnancy. During this time, of course, breast development often occurs and can proceed at a fast pace. This is how the Pill exerts its effect. But it is short-lived. Once the preparation is stopped, a quick reversal of form occurs. In fact, the breast tissue often declines to a degree which is much worse than the original picture. Do not take the Pill or, for that matter, any hormonal or chemical preparation to improve your bust measurements.

Quite a lot has been written recently about injections and plastic surgery to improve breast dimensions. What is the truth about all this?

Injecting material into the breast tissue is definitely out too. It is potentially dangerous and should never be contemplated at *any* age.

The breast is one of the commonest sites of cancer in women. By fiddling around with nature and injecting foreign substances, there could be an increased risk of serious consequences later on. The treatment of cancer of the bosom is still a highly complex (and not very satisfactory) business. It is pointless to tempt fate.

Plastic Surgery

What about plastic surgery?

The current operation of choice is to stitch a gadget called a *silastic prosthesis* into each breast, between the breast substance itself and the chest wall. This is an inert material, and once in position gives the bosom a greatly increased measurement.

Are the results satisfactory?

In many instances the results are good. However, from my

experience (covering many surgeons and many patients), many women are disappointed (and, indeed, enraged) at the final result!

Many unhappy complications have been reported. Hardness, scarring, discomfort are but a few. Many women later wished they had never embarked on the routine. (And this is anywhere from one to five years later.)

But I am not debunking the system. Of all methods, it is perhaps the best if the person believes something *must* be done.

At what age is this best carried out?

Different doctors have different views. Many believe that women in their twenties are the ones hardest hit with the breast syndrome. Therefore, they find their results with this age spectrum quite good. Improved personalities, introverts converting to extroverts, happier dispositions have all been reported as resulting from these operations.

What about girls in the under-twenty age group. Should they have these operations?

The answer is an emphatic No! Up until this age, the body is still growing. There is no certainty what will eventuate. Premature surgery could spell future serious trouble for the patient. In fact, so definite is the medical profession about this that an editorial in a recent edition of the very conservative *British Medical Journal* had this to say to doctors:

"Sometimes advice is sought because a young girl's breasts are too large or too small. They may be proving an embarrassment to her, put plastic procedures aimed at reducing or enlarging the size of the breasts should seldom, if ever, be done before the age of twenty.

"Most anomalies apparent in puberty will correct themselves before a girl becomes adult. If there is surgical interference before this age, it is impossible to predict with certainty the eventual outcome.

Advice should always be to wait until the adult form has been reached before considering cosmetic operations."[1]

It seems that some women have breasts of unequal size and tend to worry about this. Is this a serious condition?

Many women have unequal breasts, and this may continue right throughout life. It is a common condition and generally is not serious.

It is incredible how they worry about it. I've even had letters from older women who claim this fact is destroying their marriage!

If one breast is growing at an obvious and rapid rate in a young woman in relation to the other, medical opinion should be sought.

Sometimes a very rare tumor called a juvenile type fibroadenoma can occur. These are never cancerous, but are sometimes removed if they are causing gross disproportion and disfigurement.

Some Final Advice

In the overall picture, is there much that can go wrong with the developing breast in growing women?

Fortunately not. According to the experts: "Relatively few disorders complicate breast development in adolescent girls." The same experts also caution:

"Interference with the developing breast should always be avoided unless there is definite evidence that a pathological lesion (ie, some disease) is present."[2]

What then do you tell young women who still want some line of action?

After going through the various possibilities, and giving a lucid explanation of the breast and its whys and wherefores, I endeavor to place it in its right perspective. Any fellow who spurns a girl merely because her figure is not what the advertising men say it should be, is not worth knowing anyhow. You're far better off without him. Or anyone like him.

Attraction and shape are not equated in real life. Personality is what matters most. Looks are only skin deep. But grace, charm, the ability to get along with people, to be interesting, friendly, and helpful are characteristics that are ever so much more important.

This is the real issue. Spend your time developing these essential characteristics. Use the bedroom mirror, for sure. But use it in its right perspective. It's not meant to be gazed into hour after hour, with every minute body measurement studied endlessly.

Educate yourself along the lines suggested, and this will automatically make you attractive, not only to members of the opposite sex, but to people in general. Getting along with others is one of the most rewarding and essential things in life. But it must be worked on, studied, encouraged.

When these points have been mastered, suddenly your chest measurements won't matter nearly so much. Your personality will be the sparkling, cherished aspect people will be seeking.

That, in truth, is the *real* you.

REFERENCES:
1. "British Medical Journal," August 7, 1971.
2. *Ibid.*

13

Slim, Trim Figures

Now we've dealt with one aspect of the female figure, how about our spending a little time on the rest of the system?

You mean overweight in general?

Yes, overweight. Of course, a certain number suffer the opposite dilemma, underweight, but let's start with the first. More seem afflicted with an excess of poundage than a lack of it.

To be sure, you are right. In fact, overweight is one of the cardinal disorders of our affluent society. As everyone knows, the nations of the Western world are slowly digging their graves with their teeth. With an all-time record high of incomes, we eat more, we exercise less, we own more cars, buy more labor-saving devices, become more flabby, and die sooner!

While one half of the affluent world is eating itself to death, the other half is driving itself to death in the nation's modern forms of transport.

Conversely, the rest of the world (we call them "underprivileged") is rapidly starving to death!

It is all topsy-turvy! It doesn't make sense.

Obesity

You would agree that overweight is fast becoming a serious health hazard. Just what does an above-average weight mean to a person?

The immediate fact is that an overweight (or obese) person does not look so attractive as one coming within a normal range.

But there must be more to it than that!

Of course. From the clinician's point of view, good looks barely rate a mention. It is well documented that overweight people are more naturally inclined to get a long list of severe physical disorders. They are more prone to heart diseases. (Indeed, overweight is now believed to be one of the five serious causes of heart attack in modern man.) Gout, gall-bladder disease, and high blood pressure are more common in the overweight.

The overweight are more liable to accidents because they are not as agile. Massive layers of fat about the heart impede it from doing its job properly, particularly in times when extra work is essential. Abdominal organs couched in fat cannot do their task adequately either. The body temperature is upset when too much fat lies just beneath the skin.

This all sounds very sinister. But wouldn't it relate to older adults rather than teen-agers?

Not really. You see, the basic patterns of living are established very early in life. Even minor tendencies to overweight in the younger years are likely to extend into the older age segment as the years pass by. Habits learned early persist. Routines are not likely to alter merely by the passage of time. If anything, they will be accentuated.

I believe that it is very important for growing teen-agers to understand clearly the principles of eating and the inherent dangers of overweight right from the start. Only in this way

will they be on the continual lookout lest they fall victims to this common disease.

What is the cause of overweight?

There is one cause, and in the main, one cause only. Overeating! It's as simple as that. If you doubt me, just listen to what some of the diet experts have to say:

"Contrary to popular belief, there is but one true cause of obesity, namely, an intake of calories beyond the body's need in energy." That comes from an American expert.[1]

But just to be fair, let's seek an opinion from the other side of the Atlantic. Not long ago an editorial writer in the staid *British Medical Journal* declared:

"Obesity is a killing disease, and it is preventable. Fat people are fat because they eat too much. If their intake is reduced enough they will lose weight.

"The uniformly lean physique of concentration camp inmates or of the survivors of recent civil wars emphasizes this point.

"Except for the occasional patient who has a specific cause for obesity, all obese patients eat too much for their needs. The remedy is simple. They must *eat* less."[2]

Do you think there are certain cases in which people tend to be overweight?

Most definitely. Researchers have long known that mental stress will make many people eat more. If there is no ready solution to their problems, they find solace in stuffing more food into their overcrammed stomachs! Others tend to eat high-calorie foods rather than low-calorie, bulky (and filling and satisfying) ones.

This is the usual explanation of the girl who claims she has inherited her overweight predisposition. In fact, she was undoubtedly brought up on the wrong type of food and persists in eating the same foods throughout life. (In due course her children will be overweight and unsightly too!)

How easy is it to become overweight?

Too easy! In fact, merely increasing the daily food intake by 100 calories over what is actually needed by the body to carry out its normal functions, equals 700 calories in a week. This means that seventy-eight extra grams will be laid down in the body tissues as plain old-fashioned fat. In one year, this equals 4,000 grams, or converted to pounds, around nine pounds a year.

Project this into, say, a five-year pattern, and the obvious effect is startling! It equals forty-five *excess* pounds that the normal frame will not easily accomodate.

What does 100 calories equal in terms of food?

There are lots of simple ways of expressing it.

It could equal, for example, three teaspoons of butter, or one slice of bread, or two one-inch squares of fudge, or an oatmeal cookie.

However, during the adolescent years, there must be a gradual weight increase.

Of course, otherwise we wouldn't grow and would be most abnormal. Weight variations in growing teen-agers are quite wide.

To give a rough estimate of what your weight should be in relation to others, we've included a scale at the end of this chapter.

It may be used as a general guide only, and it certainly should not be taken as the absolute weight to the very pound that you should weigh. Some people are slim in build; others are more stocky. Therefore, some will naturally tend to weigh less, others to weigh more. However, my mailbag testifies to the fact that the majority of teen-agers are well aware of it if they are overweight, or normal weight, or underweight. Usually one does not have to be an expert to assess the situation.

How to Lose Weight

What is your opinion on overweight persons losing weight?

With growing teen-agers there is usually not the same need to go for *severe* diet routines as with older persons in more sedentary occupations. But general principles apply. What youngsters do in their growing years is invariably projected into their adult life. For this reason it's essential, I believe, for correct basic ideas to be firmly implanted in their minds. So if a teen-ager is obviously overweight, a reduction is the sensible thing to work for.

It is hard to tell a teen-ager to eat less. She probably becomes so ravenous that life consists of living from one meal to the next! Some goal should be established. With older girls the beauty angle is self-evident and is often enough of an incentive in itself. Good health, feeling more vital and alive, being more attractive to others, the chances of widening the sphere of friends are all possible results from becoming less bulky.

A gradual weight loss should be the aim rather than an abrupt, crash-diet routine. The latter can often give a feeling of weakness and is not recommended. Losing one pound a week often produces very satisfactory results. After all, this can add up in a few months!

What foods should be taken during a weight-reducing program?

There must be a reduction in the high-calorie, starchy foods. But meals should leave a satisfied feeling. Proteins digest slowly and remain in the stomach a long time. It's wise to include an egg at breakfast occasionally; for vegetarians, cheese, cottage cheese, nut meat, or some tasty soy product at lunch; and a repetition of this at the evening meal. These take the place of meat in the diet.

Green vegetables are of low-calorie value, but they have a

high bulk content and give a satisfying feeling merely because of this. Therefore salads are excellent in any weight-reducing regimen.

Be very careful of beverages. The sugar-filled carbonated drinks popularly available are disastrous for adding pounds. Go for either plain water or fruit juices (without sugar added).

Would you care to enumerate the type of foods that are best avoided for a person wishing to avoid putting on extra pounds?

Yes, and this can be used as a general guide.

High-fat foods: Butter, cheese (except as noted), chocolate, cream, ice cream, fat meat, fatty fish, or fish canned in oil, fried foods of any kind (eg French fries), gravies, nuts, oil, pastries, and rich salad dressings.

High-carbohydrate (starch) foods: Breads of any kind; candies, cake, cookies and biscuits; corn; products such as macaroni, noodles, spaghetti; pancakes and waffles; sweetened or dried fruits; legumes such as dried peas and beans; potatoes and sweet potatoes; honey, molasses, sugar, and syrups; rich puddings and desserts.

Beverages: All fountain drinks, including malted milks and chocolate, carbonated beverages of all kinds, rich sundaes, and all alcoholic beverages.

This seems to include every known food, doesn't it?

Not really. If you closely follow the lists, you'll find almost no mention of vegetables, apart from potatoes. Nearly all vegetables can be freely taken. Also, there is little mention of the high-protein foods. These are essential, and the majority of protein foods contain enough of the other essential ingredients of nutrition to provide us with enough calories anyhow.

I must emphasize that the above lists are to be used with common sense. Of course, it may be impossible to avoid all these items completely. But *common sense* is the general rule. Common sense applies to the food you eat, plus the amounts you eat; and you must let your common sense tell you when a halt is to be called.

Before we finish this subject, do you have any rough rule-of-thumb suggestions for the overweight?

Yes, I do. For years, I have been giving my overweight patients (irrespective of age or sex) a simple formula for effective weight reduction. It goes like this:

Avoid potatoes in all forms, bread in all forms, and sweets in all forms.

It can work like magic. If you spend five minutes contemplating this simple rule, you'll realize just what is involved!

Do you believe in drugs to assist in weight loss?

Definitely not. The amphetamines have been widely prescribed for many years. Now, fortunately, they have been banned in many countries of the world. A good thing too. Their adverse effect and dangers far outweighed any temporary benefit they may have had in the weight-losing stakes. Similarly, drugs aimed at "burning up food more rapidly" are out also.

What about exercise?

I believe that lots of exercise is essential for the growing adolescent. Some doctors believe this tends to increase weight. The appetite that exercise generates, they claim (and the increased food intake), far outweighs the calories lost due to the exercise itself.

Maybe so, but if one is attentive to the diet, there is no doubt that exercise makes for a better, more pleasing physique. It tones up the system, keeps muscles firm, the skin fresh and viable, and the cardiac and respiratory systems in top form.

New Hope for the Underweight

Could we spare a few minutes for the underweight?

Very definitely. Many young people claim their problems in life are associated with this factor. It doesn't matter what they do, they say, they cannot improve their weight. "I look like a scarecrow"; "All the boys say I'm as skinny as a rail"; "I'm just a bag of bones"; "My clothes hang on me like a coat hanger!" These are some of the plaintive comments I hear on a nonstop basis.

In principle, the *reverse* of all the good advice we offered for the overweight should see a weight increase take place with those of lesser dimensions. For example, the daily food intake must be increased. Protein is ideal for these people. There should be a considerable daily increase in this.

Some doctors believe that a vitamin deficiency may be occurring in these people, and so prescribe a multivitamin preparation each day. There are many brand names around. The majority are quite good, and many include extra minerals as well.

Would you care to outline a general type of daily food intake for these people?

Yes. I would suggest something along the following general lines:

3 to 4 cups of milk

1 cup of light cream

4 to 6 ounces of protein (eg, nut meat or similar nut or soybean-based product—meat for those who do not follow a vegetarian routine)

1 egg two or three times a week

1 serving of whole-grain bread

4 servings of vegetables including:

    1 serving of green or yellow vegetable

    2 servings of white or sweet potato, corn, or beans

1 serving of other vegetable
2 to 3 servings of fruit (including one citrus)
4 tablespoons or more of butter or fortified margarine
High-calorie foods to complete the calorie requirements of
the day include: cereal foods like macaroni, rice, noodles,
spaghetti; honey, molasses, syrups, glucose; salad dressings;
cakes, biscuits, and pastry in moderation; ice cream;
puddings and sauces.

*Do you feel that a proper medical checkup is advisable for
young people either overweight or underweight?*

Yes. In fact, many doctors advise that anyone embarking
on a diet routine should first consult her doctor for a general
physical examination. This will make certain she is not
suffering from some basic disorder which should be receiving
treatment as well. It is also wise to discuss the diet with the
physician.

Sometimes the general principles can be worked out more
accurately for an individual. This may be a better idea in
certain circumstances.

REFERENCES:
  1. Proudfit and Robinson: "Nutrition and Diet Therapy."
  2. "British Medical Journal," October 30, 1971.

WHAT IS YOUR "IDEAL" WEIGHT?

On the next page is a comprehensive range of "ideal"
weights. You will notice that from birth to seventeen years,
weight is related to age and height (Table A), and that weight
in the fifteen-to-seventeen-year bracket is extremely variable. After this age group, weight is related to height only.
Consideration is given to sex (male or female), and whether
you are of small, medium, or large physique. As many
countries are switching to "metric" measuring systems, the
tables are given in both.

AVERAGE HEIGHT AND WEIGHT FOR CHILDREN

Age Years	BOYS Height Ft.	In.	Cm.	Weight Lb.	Kg.	GIRLS Height Ft.	In.	Cm.	Weight Lb.	Kg.
Birth	1	8	50.8	7 1/2	3.4	1	8	50.8	7 1/2	3.4
1/2	2	2	66.0	17	7.7	2	2	66.0	16	7.2
1	2	5	73.6	21	9.5	2	5	73.6	20	9.1
2	2	9	83.8	26	11.8	2	9	83.8	25	11.3
3	3	0	91.4	31	14.0	3	0	91.4	30	13.6
4	3	3	99.0	34	15.4	3	3	99.0	33	15.0
5	3	6	106.6	39	17.7	3	5	104.1	38	17.2
6	3	9	114.2	46	20.9	3	8	111.7	45	20.4
7	3	11	119.3	51	23.1	3	11	119.3	49	22.2
8	4	2	127.0	57	25.9	4	2	127.0	56	25.4
9	4	4	132.0	63	28.6	4	4	132.0	62	28.1
10	4	6	137.1	69	31.3	4	6	137.1	69	31.3
11	4	8	142.2	77	34.9	4	8	142.2	77	34.9
12	4	10	147.3	83	37.7	4	10	147.3	86	39.0
13	5	0	152.4	92	41.7	5	0	152.4	98	45.5
14	5	2	157.5	107	48.5	5	2	157.5	107	48.5
15*	5	4	162.6	116	52.6	5	3	160.0	115	52.2
16*	5	6	167.6	128	58.0	5	4	162.6	118	53.5
17*	5	7	170.2	134	60.8	5	4	162.6	118	53.5

*Weight at ages 15, 16, and 17 is extremely variable.

"IDEAL" WEIGHT FOR ADULTS AGES OF 25 AND OVER[#]

Height (With Shoes) Ft. In.	Cm.	"Ideal" Weight in Pounds and Kilograms for WOMEN (For weight without shoes or clothing, subtract 2-3 pounds) Small Frame lb.	Kg.	Medium Frame lb.	Kg.	Large Frame lb.	Kg.
5 0	152.4	105-113	47.6-51.3	112-120	50.8-54.4	119-129	54.0-58.5
5 1	154.9	107-115	48.5-52.2	114-122	51.7-55.3	121-131	54.9-59.4
5 2	157.5	110-118	49.9-53.5	117-125	53.1-56.7	124-135	56.3-61.2
5 3	160.0	113-121	51.3-54.9	120-128	54.4-58.1	127-138	57.6-62.6
5 4	162.6	116-125	52.6-56.7	124-132	56.3-59.9	131-142	59.4-64.4
5 5	165.1	119-128	54.0-58.1	127-135	57.6-61.2	133-145	60.3-65.8
5 6	167.6	123-132	55.8-59.9	130-140	58.9-63.5	138-150	62.6-68.0
5 7	170.2	126-136	57.2-61.7	134-144	60.8-65.3	142-154	64.4-69.9
5 8	172.7	129-139	58.5-63.1	137-147	62.2-66.7	145-158	65.8-71.7
5 9	175.3	133-143	60.3-64.9	141-151	64.0-68.5	149-162	67.6-73.5
5 10	177.8	136-147	61.7-66.7	145-155	65.8-70.3	152-166	69.0-75.3
5 11	180.3	139-150	63.1-68.0	148-158	67.1-71.7	155-169	70.3-76.7
6 0	182.9	141-153	64.0-69.4	151-163	68.5-73.9	160-174	72.6-78.9

Height (With Shoes) Ft. In.	Cm.	"Ideal" Weight in Pounds and Kilograms for MEN (For weight without shoes or clothing, subtract 5-6 pounds) Small Frame lb.	Kg.	Medium Frame lb.	Kg.	Large Frame lb.	Kg.
5 2	157.5	116-125	52.6-56.7	124-133	56.3-60.3	131-142	59.4-64.4
5 3	160.0	119-128	54.0-58.1	127-136	57.6-61.7	133-144	60.3-65.3
5 4	162.6	122-132	55.3-59.9	130-140	58.9-63.5	137-149	62.1-67.6
5 5	165.1	126-136	57.1-61.7	134-144	60.8-65.3	141-153	63.9-69.4
5 6	167.6	129-139	58.5-63.1	137-147	62.2-66.7	145-157	65.8-71.2
5 7	170.2	133-143	60.3-64.9	141-151	64.0-68.5	149-162	67.6-73.5
5 8	172.7	136-147	61.7-66.7	145-156	65.8-70.8	153-166	69.4-75.3
5 9	175.3	140-151	63.5-68.5	149-160	67.6-72.6	157-170	71.2-77.1
5 10	177.8	144-155	65.3-70.3	153-164	69.4-74.4	161-175	73.0-79.4
5 11	180.3	148-159	67.1-72.1	157-168	71.2-76.2	165-180	74.8-81.7
6 0	182.9	152-164	69.0-74.4	161-173	73.0-78.5	169-185	76.7-83.9
6 1	185.4	157-169	71.2-76.7	166-178	75.3-80.7	174-190	78.9-86.2
6 2	188.0	163-175	73.9-79.4	171-184	77.6-83.5	179-196	81.2-88.9
6 3	190.5	168-180	76.2-81.7	176-189	79.8-85.7	184-202	83.5-91.6

#For ages 18 to 25 - approximate "ideal" weights can be calculated by subtracting 1.0 lb. (0.5 Kg.) for each year of age less than 25 years.

(Courtesy of the Metropolitan Life Insurance Company)

14

How to Make People Like You

What do you think is the most important thing in the world?

That's a wide-range question. It could embrace anything or everything. There are hundreds of "most important things" in life, so it depends on what facet you have in mind.

Look at it from the point of being happy and content.

I think your question is probably your answer as well.

Being happy and content and having peace of mind is tremendously important. Maybe this forms the greatest aspect of life in itself. So many people are unhappy and perpetually dissatisfied and gloomy and filled with despair.

How can we be happy and content and achieve inner peace?

I am sure there is no simple rule. I believe it is a combination of many different thoughts.

For example, maintaining good health is very important to keeping mentally fit. In turn, this will help us achieve inner peace and happiness.

Remembering the simple basics of living assists also. I believe in the golden rule. If we do to others the things we'd like them to do to us, this in turn can yield phenomenal rewards and play an important part in keeping us happy and contented. Thinking of the other person and his needs before our own is the essential ingredient here. The more we concentrate on ourselves, the more self-centered and selfish we inevitably become. I am sure this does us very little good in the overall concept of life.

What about friends?

Oh, that is very important. In fact, having lots of friends is one of the uppermost joys of life. What could be worse than having nobody who loved you or cared about you? Can you imagine anything more devastating?

Do you think it is important that young people choose the right occupation in life?

Yes, I do. But this is often easier said than done. There is nothing so rewarding as "job satisfaction." It means that when you work, you're really "playing." Work and relaxation then become synonymous. There is nothing quite so vitalizing as to enjoy the manner in which you spend your working and relaxing hours.

If one virtually equals the other, so much the better.

But I'm sure you have something in mind with all these queries you're throwing up at me all at once. Come, now, what's your little plan?

I'd like to take a few of these facets and examine them in detail. Not too much detail; but maybe some general guidelines can be worked out that will give our readers a few starting points for further thinking.

This sounds perfectly reasonable. Where do we start?

You just mentioned the topic of friends. Let's take the word in the broad sense. Friends in general–not particularly boy-girl friendships. Basically, how can you make people like you?

I think we're all striving to this end, whether we realize it or not. We all feel the inherent need for affiliation with other humans. We're a race of "community livers," and the need for close companionship right throughout life is very important.

Do you have a workable formula for making people like you?

There is not any hard and fast system. Rather there are only the more general ideas. Some of these could be set out like this:

1. Helpfulness

There is nothing much nicer than having someone around who is willing to help you. This is most pronounced when you're in need. Of course this may vary from time to time and from one set of circumstances to another. But if you are willing and ready to lend a friendly hand to help others, you'll never want for friends. You will notice, though, that there are miserable creatures who will take unfair advantage of this. But in the overall picture, this way you'll find more true friends than phonies out for tangible benefits. In due course the wheel of life turns around, you know. One day (often when you're least expecting it) someone will help *you*.

2. Thoughtfulness

The world in general is too busy thinking of itself (and its worries and perplexities) to care much about anyone else. But if you take the time and make the effort to think a bit about others, you are guaranteed a superabundance of firm and long-standing friendships.

Thoughtful people are usually helpful people. The two go hand in hand. Think of the other person first. But THINK! It is mentally refreshing and, oh, so rewarding, even though you may have a difficult time at first.

3. The Other Person's Point of View

There are huge numbers of people in the world who are always right. (Sad to say, but the older we become, often the more single-eyed we become and refuse to see anyone else's viewpoint but our own. And how wrong we can often be!)

Put yourself in the other person's shoes as often as you can. Look at situations and circumstances from his position. This will often throw a completely different light on a set of circumstances. It will often answer a series of questions you had in mind about a person. Maybe you didn't like someone—until you discovered that she had many problems and had a good reason to act the way she did.

"Empathy" is the popular word for this. This simply means "the power of entering into another person's personality, and imaginatively living his experiences." It can make a whole world of friends if you're prepared to let yourself work this way. I can assure you it pays off in the number of new, true friends you'll acquire without any effort at all.

4. Cheerfulness

Do you like associating with people who have a perpetual scowl on their faces? Or maybe a scowl in their voices?

I would prefer to run a mile. Many people just cannot look or sound cheerful, no matter what. And have you noticed the number of friends they accumulate? It's not hard to count them. They have very few. And they are not likely to collect many on the journey through life when they act this way either.

Happiness and cheerfulness breed happiness and cheerfulness. Surprisingly enough, if you speak to an unhappy character, and really try to be pleasant, in due course she will come your way. In fact, it is an interesting (and quite rewarding) little pastime—if you have the time and patience.

Winning over some cranky sourpuss can be really a mentally

exhilarating experience. I've done it on numerous occasions. In fact, in my job it makes life (and treatment) ever so much more successful and simple. I never fail to get a mental lift if someone finally cracks a smile and starts acting like a happy human being after having been getting around as though the world were about to end tomorrow!

5. Sympathy

Sympathy isn't only for funeral occasions. It's an essential ingredient in the friend-winning campaign and must be pulled out of the bag of tricks each day. If you can show a genuine sympathy for others with problems, you are guaranteed to have more friends about than you can possibly cope with.

Once again, the world is full of greedy people who care for themselves and nobody else. To find a person who is understanding and sympathetic is really something out of this world. There are so many occasions when you can show this very human side of your character. It is invariably well rewarded. The very person who needs a little sympathetic understanding is more than likely the one who will reciprocate when the wheel turns full circle and you find yourself in a position needing a little tender understanding too.

6. Interest

Taking an interest in others is one of the most rewarding ways of discovering friends.

Many people are so wrapped up in their own little world that they haven't the time to bother with anyone else. Just check out their circle of friends. It is virtually nonexistent.

Showing interest in others has a happy way of yielding rich dividends in the bank of life. Not only do you form a wide circle of true friends, but in turn you'll discover that your friends are taking a true interest in you as well. There is nothing quite so exhilarating as having someone evince an interest in you and your activities, whatever you are doing.

7. The Other Person's Feelings

Being aware of the other person's feelings is a surefire way of attracting friends and making yourself more popular.

Just watch with your own circle of school friends or college acquaintances. Some take a fiendish delight in making another person feel small and embarrassed whenever and wherever the opportunity arises. The opportunities, of course, are unlimited for this hateful pastime. The really professional ones can turn almost any incident back on a person and make him or her squirm and wish the roof would fall in. But the one who attracts true companionship is the one who does exactly the opposite.

If there is an obvious way of embarrassing a friend (or foe—it doesn't matter which), the true-blue friend winner will reverse the situation and use it to bolster up the morale and spirits of the person headed for disaster.

8. Share a Little, Give a Little

The person who is wanted most of all is the one willing to share a little and give a little. It doesn't really matter what. Maybe it is time. Or his or her talent. Maybe it is a book someone wants or a little affection.

I have lots of aged persons under my care. Nothing gives these dear old souls greater pleasure than for me (or anyone else, for that matter) to stop and spend some time with them.

Maybe there is nothing much to talk about (although this is really not much of a problem). It is the fact that someone has taken the time to give them something when the rest of the world is passing them that gives them intense pleasure. But this need not be relegated to old persons. It applies to all human beings, irrespective of the age spectrum.

Sharing around is just great. Those who share the most gain the most—not only in the immediate accumulation of more friends, but frequently in other ways as well. In due course when *you* need something badly, there is invariably someone around who is willing to reciprocate in the way you did initially. This is certainly worth bearing in mind.

9. Willingness

Ever asked someone to do something, and the person carries out the instruction with a snarl and a sour face? How does it grab you?

Now what about the reverse? Do you snap and snarl and look sour and disgruntled when certain tasks come your way?

Willingness is one of the greatest attributes in this world. It breeds friends faster than any other single cause. Why not bear it well in mind? Try it as an experiment if you tend to doubt my words.

10. The Golden Rule

To sum up all this getting friends business, I feel I must repeat the short text I started off with. That's the "golden rule." It really sums up the entire concept of living, of gaining friends, of being at peace with the world and all mankind.

"Do for others what you want them to do for you."

It doesn't matter how you phrase it. It means the same. The chief essential, of course, is to try to put it into your daily living. Not just for a day or two, but on a nonstop basis. There is no doubt that the payoff is tremendously worthwhile. What you pump into life will inevitably come back. Not one-fold, not two-fold; but one-hundred-fold!

Believe me, it is true!

15

This Vital Chapter Tells You --

How to Develop Poise and Self-confidence
How to Develop Talent
How to Develop the Art of Conversation
How to Solve Problems
How to Pass Exams
How to Succeed

How can a person develop self-confidence?

For some this is simple. Indeed, some people are so extroverted in their approach to life that it's almost sickening! Conversely, others are born (it seems) with an inherent withdrawn, introspective nature. They seem to lack drive. They are shy, timid, easily embarrassed, and find it a burden to express themselves and to meet others. Indeed, you may be interested to know that there are ever so many more of the latter kind of people around than the former.

Does that cheer you up a little, if you are one of the endless army of people plagued by a lack of self-confidence?

I believe there are a few clear-cut ways for persons in this

190

second category to improve themselves to the point where they can develop just the right amount of self-confidence.

Of course, this is not the only payoff. Once this has been achieved, all the other bonus extras that are freely added are just out of this world.

What do you mean by this?

A person who is self-confident has many other attributes. Usually she is poised at all times, invariably well-mannered, and full of vitality.

She tends to develop other talents as well. In fact, there often seems no end to the number and variety of talents a girl can build up, bit by bit. In due course she will become a good conversationalist, and in turn this will make her an attractive, friendly hostess.

She will become good at meeting people, and will develop her own individual charm and personality that will be attractive to an ever-widening circle of people. Therefore, she will tend to acquire more and more friends; and, as we have already seen, this is one of the most satisfying things this world has to offer.

What are the initial steps to acquiring self-confidence?

To my way of thinking, there are two great questions involved. Fortunately, with a little practice, the overwhelming majority of people (of any age) can develop these, irrespective of how "backward" they believe themselves to be.

The First Step

What is the first one?

SET A GOAL.

This may sound so simple that you'll say, "It's a waste of time." But, I assure you that nothing is farther from the truth. Now, by "goal" I do not mean one simple goal. Instead, I mean a series of them.

It is important that the first goal be a relatively simple one. It may be that you've been invited to a party. At parties you are invariably shy and tend to hide away in a corner by yourself, merely because you do not know anyone very well. Well, the very next time you're invited somewhere, your "goal" for that event is to mix around. Determine in your mind you'll really have a ball that night. Decide you'll speak to every person present. During the week or two preceding the party, make a list of the things you'll talk about. Go over this each day until you have a whole string of possible topics and talking points well in mind.

Scan the papers each day, watch TV for a while, tune in to the radio, keep your eyes and ears open for interesting current topics. Finally, when the party does roll around, instead of being stuck away by yourself, you're all set to reach your goal of speaking to everyone present.

Bit by bit as you do this, you'll circulate. Just as you radiate your own opinions and personality, in turn others will be caught up in this and will return what you are giving. This way you'll not only have a great time, but you'll most probably make more friends than you dreamed possible. And more important, goal number one will have been reached.

What happens then?

Then it's on toward goal number two!

I do not know what that might be. It could be related to schoolwork, passing an important test, going for a job, trying to get to know a particular person. It is a case of setting up a definite, attainable goal, then working out a modus operandi for achieving it.

In a very short time, you'll find your life is becoming studded with goals. It soon becomes a routine matter. Each day will have its particular set of goals. In fact, often there may be several for the day. There will be others for the week,

for the month, for the year. Finally, you'll find that there are lifetime goals.

But as you achieve your goals, they become milestones. If you let defeat and gloom and despair take over, of course your milestones could be converted into millstones! That must *never* happen.

As you achieve your hourly, daily, weekly, monthly, yearly goals, so the feeling of self-confidence will become more firmly entrenched.

Before you know it, the old feelings of insecurity and lack of confidence will vanish completely. Oh, for sure, they will return from time to time. That is only natural. But if they do come knocking at your door, you must rapidly throw them out. The sooner this is done the better.

Goals, goals, and more goals is the aim. And successfully reaching those goals is the important achievement.

The Second Step

What is the second part?

THINK POSITIVELY.

This is intimately combined with your "goal-achieving system." When a goal is set, you must convince yourself that you *will* make the grade.

For this reason, especially in the early stages, do not make your goals too hard to achieve or too time-consuming. Far better to have a series of fairly small, easily obtainable ones than one very difficult hurdle to surmount.

Achievement gives added zest and builds up the confidence, and this in turn will give you an inherent ability to achieve the next one, which should be a little more difficult. Tell yourself you can make the grade, that your system is built of the right stuff, that you are filled with stamina and determination. If you really believe in yourself and your ability to get things done, nothing in this wide world can stop you.

You see, each of us has a brain. And that brain consists of two important parts.

First there is the conscious part. This is the part by which we carry out our daily duties. It is that part which gives us the awareness of what is going on about us. We live and act from hour to hour by virtue of the conscious part of our brain.

Second there is also another part, maybe as important or even more important. This the subconscious part. This is a vital part of our nervous system. Indeed, many believe that it forms an even more important basic part of our bodies than the conscious part of our brain system. Not only does this automatically control all our body functions, but it is the storehouse or memory bank of the system. Indeed, it is really a human computer. Here untold millions of facts are stored away in our memory banks. We are often completely unaware of them but that doesn't matter.

Like the mechanical computers, the human ones have one vital thing in common. They will store only (and remember, and hence later recall) the data that is fed into them! Now, this may not sound very important. That is, until you look at it in a bit more detail. For you see that the more "positive" data you inject into your computer, the more "positive data" will be regurgitated when the need arises. Pump in negative factors, and negative factors will be returned. Get the general picture?

Therefore, if you keep telling your built-in computer system that you are determined to succeed in life, or reach any particular goal, then succeed you must. You've been programmed to succeed.

Correct. Of course sensible people will go along and make every additional effort to reach their goals. If special study or special work is involved, they will attend to this. But this is likewise fed into the memory bank. It all mixes up there in some unknown way. The end product is a feedback of success unlimited!

Crazy? Am I talking through my hat? Not really. I have seen the system work on so many occasions that nothing now will convince me otherwise. Why not try it and see for yourself? It is absolutely incredible how success and achievement will come your way. In fact, I'd go so far as to say that you *cannot fail* once you fully convince yourself that this system is for you.

Do you really mean this?

I do. Failure becomes an impossibility! This system works equally well with the topic we started off with: developing self-confidence. For this it is simply the greatest. But it works with equal success in nearly every other facet of life you care to mention.

It may be applied to gaining more friends. It can be used to help you become a good conversationalist or a good student, to passing exams, finding yourself a boyfriend, developing talent, choosing the right calling in life. You name it, the system is excellent!

But there is one other important aspect to this as well. *What's that?*

There must be a starting point. Nobody is going to *make* you use this system. It is purely voluntary. It is up to you. My advice is to commence right away, this very day. There is no time like the present. Put it off until tomorrow, and tomorrow has a funny habit of never arriving. It is always another twenty-four hours away. Why not make the start *this very minute?*

Get a pencil and paper right now. I'll hold everything for ten seconds while you do just that.

Something for You to Do

Time's up. Are you talking to me or our readers? Or are you talking to both?

I am talking to you both.

You have your pencil and paper in your hand? Now write down your first goal.

It doesn't matter what it is as far as I'm concerned. Only it is best if it is something that has been worrying you lately. Preferably something you've found a little difficult (but not *too* hard). Remember this is goal number one. Take it easy. Have you written that down?

Yes.

Now tell yourself that you intend to succeed with that goal. Nothing in this wide world will prevent you from securing this in a reasonable time.

Now underneath this write down several ways in which you will achieve your goal.

List them right under each other. Go on, write them down, *now*. See how easy it really is once you make a start?

I want you to read and reread this list several times during the day. Each time you read the list you tell yourself again that you are determined you will succeed in reaching this goal, come what may.

You will positively *think* yourself into success.

When you go to bed at night, read the list again, and as you lie down to sleep, the list of items you've written down will roll around in your subconscious. Next morning when you wake up, you'll be amazed at how many of the items you've listed seem to have become clearer, seem to have a ready-made answer that you hadn't considered earlier. Why, even the goal itself may have been solved. Do you get the general idea?

I think we all do.

One Last Thing

There is one other aspect which does a tremendous lot in reinforcing this method of achieving success. I have left it till last, not because it is the least in importance, but because I feel it is the most important.

In any system like this you'll invariably achieve greater and quicker and more satisfying success if you take God into your confidence as well. Praying is not an old-fashioned practice any longer. The rich and the famous and the successful regularly use the system.

It is far nicer having a partner in things than going them all alone. And what better partner than God Himself?

Outline to Him your goals, your hopes, your fears, your ambitions. Ask Him to give you assistance, courage, determination, and I can absolutely guarantee you that success will come your way even more quickly than you had hoped.

Of course, when this does occur, do not forget to give Him sincere thanks. I am sure God appreciates being thanked, just as does a human being. It's nice to be remembered.

Drugs and the Teen-ager

It's a well-recognized fact that more and more teen-agers are becoming involved in the drug-taking system. How widespread do you think this is?

According to the experts who spend their time poring over facts and figures, "one-third of all United States schools have a 'serious' drug problem."[1]

In Australia "at least 50 percent of the school population in the twelve- to sixteen-year age bracket are well aware of drugs and drug-taking, kicks, and all associated detail."[1]

How do young people get hold of drugs?

It's very easy. They're available everywhere. In fact, sooner or later, nearly every growing teen-ager will be offered drugs in one form or another!

How does the system operate?

Most commonly, it goes something like this: Someone approaches you. Probably it is a school pal.

"Look here," says your school pal; "I've got some caps." (Displays some brightly colored capsules or tablets, with obvious pride.) "What about having one? *I* did. Made me feel great. Gives you a real lift. Makes you feel great. Won't hurt you. Look at me. *I'm* all right. You know me. I'm your friend. Go on, give it a try. I can get some more after this. No problem at all!''

It is as simple as that. Or alternatively, someone might approach you at a party, on the street, at the beach, at a swimming pool, in public transport, at a picnic, at a sports event. There will be the same general line of talk—capsules, or tablets, or maybe the idea of an injection.

There is talk of this ''making you feel wonderful, able to study better, think clearer, having a marvelous sensation.'' It's always a positive story of attraction and appeal.

What is the best line of counterattack once you've been approached?

Sensible people will immediately be suspicious. Taking drugs is a sinister experiment. Once the first fateful step has been taken, it inevitably leads from one point to another in a general downhill direction. Those who have watched countless people reach the bottom rung of the ladder advise extreme caution.

Teen-agers should resist any approach or friendliness by an unknown person. Under NO circumstances take any pill, capsule, or injection from a stranger.

If the possibility opens to you, keep moving. Don't stop and talk. Keep moving. Be especially careful at the types of functions I've mentioned.

What are the most likely drugs a young person would be offered?

This will vary enormously. It varies from town to town, state to state, country to country. It depends on the current availability of drugs at any given time in any given place. The amphetamines are still popular. In many countries these have now been totally banned.

But there are still supplies fairly widely distributed. This is the well-known "speed" or "uppers."

For many years, the amphetamines were widely prescribed as an appetite depressant and were used to help overweight people lose excess pounds. Just how many people became habituated to the powerful drug in this way is still unknown.

The barbiturates (downers) are used in medicine as a nerve settler. These are often sold by drug peddlers, but they are not very popular.

What about marijuana?

Marijuana is extremely popular. Right now it's riding on the crest of the wave. It goes by various colloquial names. "Grass" and "pot" are two of the common ones.

Hashish is a clear resin that is derived from the plant, but it is said to be up to ten times more potent. Actually the word "hashish" is Arabic for "assassin." Once it was believed that it gave the user a violent desire to kill. This is not true, but the name persists.

Marijuana comes from a plant that grows freely in many places. But supplies ordinarily do not come from local sources. In Western countries, most marijuana is illegally imported. It is widely distributed and readily available.

Pot (like speed) is not physically addictive and for this reason there has been widespread agitation over the past few years to have it legalized.

It has no therapeutic use in modern medicine. It contains a variety of properties common to stimulants, sedatives, tranquilizers, hallucinogens, and narcotics. Its effect on driving performance indicates its deleterious effects. These are very similar to those found when drivers have had a moderate intake of alcohol.

In the social setting, the "fifth dimension" is the one that gives greatest appeal. Subjective effects such as alteration in time (it seems longer), space perception, euphoria, relaxation, a sense of well-being and disinhibition, dulling of attention, fragmentation of thought, an altered sense of identity, exaggerated laughter and increased suggestibility, the feeling of a heightened artistic ability (but without any objective evidence of this) reveal something of the potency of this drug.

The experts are quite convinced that "cannabis [marijuana] is a potent drug having as wide a capacity as alcohol to alter mood, judgment, and functional ability." Other authorities are quite definite that "cannabis is a dangerous drug."[2]

Another appealing factor, of course, is that smoking a drug seems so simple, so easy. It does not appear to be nearly so serious as injecting something into the body with a needle.

A major fear with marijuana is that its long-term effects are yet quite unknown. Many experts believe that there could be serious repercussions. Only time will unravel this aspect.

What about LSD?

Short for lysergic acid diethylamide, LSD is a potent chemical that was developed by a Swiss chemical researcher seeking a new cure for migraine headaches. He hit upon "acid" and enjoyed a fantastic "trip" home from work that night on his bicycle. In a moment he realized he'd unleashed a genie. But it was an evil genie.

LSD is an extremely potent drug. It gives a distorted picture of the outside world, but its use is very widespread. It is readily available.

"Hard Drugs"

What are the "hard drugs"?

These are the really serious ones and are "danger plus." They include the narcotics.

The key danger is that the body soon comes to depend on their use. This rapidly develops. Then, if it is decided to discontinue them, "withdrawal symptoms" set in. These symptoms are terrible in the extreme.

Therefore, people on the "hard drugs" tend to seek more and more supplies. Addicts go to any lengths to secure them. The drugs are usually given by injection, either by the person himself or by an accomplice.

Heroin is the greatest worry. It was used medically at one time, but now it is completely banned. "It is believed that nobody can resist becoming addicted to heroin if it is given for any lenth of time."[1]

Other drugs are also in this category. Pethidine, morphine, and others closely related are taken by the addict. These are often legally used by doctors to alleviate severe pain. They are given under proper medical supervision and for short periods only.

What does it feel like to have a shot of heroin?

According to those who have been through the mill, the initial sensation (or "flash" as it's termed) is remarkably pleasurable. However, the sting comes in that a gradually increasing amount is needed each time to secure the same initial sensation.

As the amount increases, so does the cost, and so does the tolerance to the drug. Most addicts resort to crime to raise the necessary funds to continue their habit.

Why Not Legalize it?

If marijuana causes no outward sign of disease, why the concern about it?

There are many reasons. The individual who takes the drug is often from a home in which problems exist. Quite often he takes it "in spite of everyone and everything." Frequently it is his way of showing his rebellion to the world, his friends, or his parents. Many surveys carried out with university students indicate the same findings. Usually he is involved with other drugs as well. Alcohol and tobacco are almost constant.

But it may lead on to a desire for more potent chemicals, wherein lies the real danger. Of course, once this becomes established, the chances of rehabilitation diminish greatly (and rapidly).

Is there a "drug personality"?

It is interesting to note that most drug takers are not interested in religion and have seldom been church attenders. Many come from homes where parental unity was lacking. Usually initial supplies came from a friend.

Most persons using the drug realize they are doing something which is illegal, but this does not worry them. Many are quite intellectual and attain good results at the university, and indeed are intellectually openminded and extroverts.

What happens when the "hard stuff" is started?

Disaster at this stage is just around the corner. Indeed, if heroin is the drug of choice (often this is the next step), it is merely a matter of time before final and ultimate destruction.

The addict soon loses interest in his usual surroundings, family and friends, hobbies, or work. He becomes untidy, disheveled, and unkempt. He associates with like souls. The one and only delight is the "next fix." Infections run high, for he ceases to care about sterility of the instruments used for the injections. Often incorrect doses are given, and this in itself has caused many deaths due to overdose.

He'll resort to any measure to obtain supplies. Crime, including theft and even violence, is part of his routine to guarantee continuity of the drugs.

What is being done for addicts?

Various governmental agencies are doing their best. But the drug addict is not interested in seeking help, for help is not what he personally desires.

Drug squads endeavor to eradicate the problem, but they face a mountainous, almost impossible, task. Both federal and private centers try to rehabilitate those addicts that come to their notice, but it seems that they cannot hope to cope with the monumental problem.

What is the answer, then?

There is only one answer. Every teen-ager should be aware of the inherent dangers that drug taking embraces. Under no circumstances get on the road. It's a one-way street to doom.

Read all you can about the problem. Discuss it with your friends. Fortify yourself and be prepared to knock it the moment you see it on your doorstep.

Do not get involved. Saying Yes the first time could be the start on the track to eternal physical and mental ruin.

Can you suggest further reading on this subject?

Yes. An excellent book devoted entirely to this topic is *The Creeping Madness.* Write to Narcotics Education, Inc., PO Box 4390, Washington, DC 20012, for information about this book and other material available on this vital topic.

Is Tobacco as Bad as They Say?

What about cigarette smoking? This is a kind of drug taking too, isn't it?

The use of tobacco in any form is drug taking!

Indeed, alcohol and tobacco are the two drugs most widely abused by our society.[2]

For some strange and entirely unaccountable reason, both alcohol and tobacco are socially acceptable forms of drug taking! While takers of other drugs can receive stiff legal sentences, no such charge awaits the habitual addict of tobacco or alcohol unless he breaks the law in addition to his smoking or drinking.

How widespread is smoking?

It is virtually pandemic.

The United States has the dubious honor of leading the world in per capita consumption. "The office of the Surgeon General reported Jan. 10 [1974] that cigarette consumption in the U.S. had increased to 583 billion from 524 billion in 1963, the year the Surgeon General made public a study warning of the health hazards of smoking. However the Surgeon General's office tied the higher consumption to increased population, as per capita consumption declined from 4,345 per year in 1963 to 4,130 in 1973."[3]

A 1971 report for the United Kingdom, according to the Tobacco Manufacture Standing Committee, indicated that "72 percent of men, and 39 percent of women are regular smokers."[4]

In fact, these figures are probably out of date by now, for the habit is increasing by leaps and bounds, and it is virtually impossible to print up-to-date figures that are not surpassed before the ink is dry.

What is the major hazard of cigarette smoking?

The three major smoking-related diseases are (1) lung cancer, (2) chronic bronchitis and emphysema, and (3) coronary heart disease.

Indeed, the effect of smoking on the heart is perhaps the most startling discovery of modern times. That it is a major killer and one increasing at a terrifying pace is now undisputed in reliable medical quarters.

In Great Britain, where intensive studies have been carried out, it has been shown that more people are dying suddenly at a progressively younger age than ever before. This is directly linked with cigarette smoking.

In a recent ten-year study it has been shown that in the 35- to 44-year age group, coronary artery disease has increased by 50 percent! This is alarming, to say the least.[5] But it affects the young just as surely. A study of 300 American soldiers killed in the Korean war, with an average age of twenty-two years, showed that there was well-advanced heart disease in 12 percent of them.[5]

Coronary artery disease is the biggest single killer in the community. About 40 percent of deaths are due to it, and the figure is rapidly rising.

It frequently attacks without warning, and death can occur within an hour and often less. People literally "drop dead in their tracks."

How can these diseases be checked?

Doctors everywhere are quite adamant. Stop smoking and the chances of longer life rapidly increase.

At the Second World Conference on Smoking and Health held recently in London (1971), smoking was called "the most preventable of modern epidemics."[6]

Many countries are in the process of banning cigarette advertising. However, there is a far simpler solution to the problem: DO NOT START IN THE FIRST PLACE.

If you don't start, you'll never miss it. I do not smoke, never have, and very likely never will. I recommend this procedure to all my readers whatever their age.

If a person has commenced, my advice is: Give it up before it gains such a strong hold that breaking the habit becomes very difficult.

If you find you haven't the willpower alone, turn to our chapter entitled "This Vital Chapter Tells You—" It's all about goals in life and positive thinking. This, plus the added help of God, will definitely assist you with your problem.

But give it up this day—before it is too late, and before the

Class of Chemical	Drug	Medical Use	Potential Physical Dependence	Potential for Psychological Dependence
NARCOTICS	Heroin	Illegal to use	Yes	Yes
	Morphine	To relieve pain	Yes	Yes
	Codeine	To relieve pain, diarrhea, or severe cough	Yes	Yes
	Paragoric	To relieve cough	Yes	Yes
	Pethidine	To relieve pain	Yes	Yes
	Methadone	To relieve pain	Yes	Yes
SEDATIVES	Barbiturates and Tranquilizers	To induce sleep, sedation, treatment of epilepsy and high blood pressure	Yes	Yes
	Bromides	Limited use for sedation and to induce sleep	Yes	Yes
	Alcohol	Limited medical use	Yes	Yes
	Glue	No medical use	Unknown	Yes
	Nicotine	No medical use	Yes (with very high intake)	Yes
STIMULANTS	Amphetamines	Strictly limited medical use	No	Yes
	Cocaine	Local anesthetic	No	Yes
	Caffeine	Mild stimulant	No	Yes
	APC	To reduce mild pain and fever	No	Yes
HALLUCINOGENS	STP	No medical use	No	Yes
	LSD	Minimal psychiatric use	No	Yes
	DMT	No medical use	No	Yes
	Mescaline	No medical use	No	Yes
	Psilocybin	No medical use	No	Yes
HALLUCINOGEN INTOXICANT	Marijuana	No present medical use	No	Yes

mediate Effects	Long-term Effects
rcotics reduce physical and psychological sensitivity, sulting in a loss of contact with reality. Sense of euphoria d reduced fear, tension and anxiety. Reduced physical tivity, drowsiness or sleep. Pinpoint pupils; constipation, usea, and vomiting in some individuals. High doses may use unconsciousness, coma, and sometimes death.	Withdrawal symptoms range from mild yawning, perspiration—tremors, loss of appetite and insomnia—to severe diarrhea, vomiting, muscle pain, and weight loss. Self-injection with unsterile syringes can lead to hepatitis, multiple abscesses, and septicemia. The commonest cause of death among individuals using narcotics is an overdose of the drug. With tolerance the drug dependent will require larger and larger doses to achieve effect. This becomes expensive, and addicts of long standing often turn to crime to maintain their habits.
	Convulsions, which may follow withdrawal, can be fatal—cause of many accidental deaths and suicides.
nall doses reduce tensions, anxiety, and inhibitions, re- lting in a feeling of relaxation, drowsiness, or stupor. rger doses may produce slurred speech, staggering it, sluggish reactions, erratic emotionality, and ulti- ately sleep.	Bromides accumulate in the body causing symptoms such as constant headache, irritability, and confusion.
	Continued heavy use may lead to DT, irreversible brain damage, heart damage, and cirrhosis of the liver.
ove effects also apply to glue sniffing; sniffers may also ffer from nausea, inflamed nostrils, lips, and eyes.	With continued glue sniffing, red and white blood cells are reduced. May be degenerative changes in heart muscle, central nervous system, and liver.
	Long-term heavy smoking may result in lung cancer, chronic bronchitis, and other respiratory complaints. Long-term abuse of nicotine may lead to high blood pres- sure and heart disease.
creased blood pressure and pulse rate. Decreased igue; elation and self-confidence and an increase in tivity. Dilated pupils, tremors, talkativeness, disorienta- n, hallucinations, and increased perspiration and urina- n. Severe depression frequently follows as the effect of e stimulant wears off.	A high degree of tolerance develops, and self- administered dosage increases greatly. Psychiatric dis- turbance may occur.
evation of mood suppression of hunger, decreased igue. If administered intravenously, may cause a peak of nsation. May also cause sensory hallucinations, eg, im- inary insects crawling under the skin.	The mucous membranes around the nose may become damaged from continued inhalation of the drug. Also diges- tive disorders, emaciation, sleeplessness, and sensory hal- lucinations.
sually well tolerated in small amounts. It generally in- eases alertness and combats mild fatigue. May cause somnia, rapid pulse, and increased urination.	Caffeine is harmful to people with heart damage.
verdose of APC may cause gastric upset.	Continual abuse of APC may result in anemia, kidney dam- age, and stomach ulcers.
usions and hallucinations (eg, colored lights, ychedelic patterns, geometric designs, music, voices, nsations of warmth). May be an increased awareness of lor and colored objects, a seeming awareness of internal gans and processes of the body. Depersonalization; re- ious and mystical experiences; increased suggestibil- ; enhanced recall or memory; abrupt and frequent anges of mood. Panic states of severe anxiety (freak- ts) sometimes occur. Physical effects include pupil dila- n and sweating.	Little known about the long-term effects. Chromosomal damage has been reported by some scientists, but the evidence is still in the balance. May precipitate psychosis, attempted suicide, depression, and "flashback" experi- ence.
tial stimulation which fades into relaxation accompanied euphoria, talkativeness, laughter, sensations of floating, seemingly increased esthetic appreciation and in- eased ability to communicate. There may be striking llucinations and illusions such as the slowing down of ne. This initial response may be followed by drowsiness sleep. Physical effects are decreased muscular coordi- tion, clumsiness, dry mouth, dizziness, bloodshot eyes, nger, occasionally nausea and vomiting, increased uri- ation, and sometimes diarrhea.	Little is known about long-term effects of marijuana. Con- sistent usage may lead to generalized fatigue, extended patterns of sleep, and general apathy. Recent research suggests the active principle is hallucinogenic and may have long-term ill effects if used heavily.

sinister tentacles of destruction get a foothold in your system.

Can you offer further reading for any reader who wants more facts on smoking and its effects on the system?

One of the best documented booklets available anywhere in the world is the one written by a Committee of the Royal College of Physicians of London and entitled ''Smoking and Health Now.'' [Printed 1971 by Pitman Medical and Scientific Publishing Co.] It is an updated edition of their first book, ''Smoking and Health,'' which appeared in 1962 and was one of the first authoritative reports on the effect of tobacco on health ever to appear.

Anyone reading this dramatic book would never smoke again. In fact, so marked was the effect in England when the second volume appeared that a reduction of 6 percent in the national smoking habits took place, and this was still maintained twelve months later.[7]

''Al. Cohol'' Is Not My Friend

Let's have a brief look at alcohol. What are your general views on this?

Like its counterpart, tobacco, alcohol is one of the ''socially acceptable'' drugs of addiction.

Just why it is given the official stamp of approval the world over when other drugs of less severe consequences have stiff sentences imposed on the users is not clear. Maybe it's because so many of the lawmakers would then be potential lawbreakers!

In a recent medical publication sent to doctors throughout the world on acceptable addictions, the writer stated: ''Alcoholism abounds with paradoxes. It is a far more common and serious problem than other forms of drug dependence in developed countries. It is a notably toxic, habit-forming drug.

"There are a third of a million alcoholics in Britain, and several million in the United States. Alcoholism is a major public health problem of epidemic proportions. Yet nobody knows precisely its cause, much less how to prevent or treat it."[8]

Why are alcoholic beverages so popular in society?

There is little doubt. The fact that alcohol reduces inhibitions, relaxes the nervous system, impairs judgment, and dulls finer sensibilities are undoubtedly the major reasons for its unparalleled popularity.

Be present on the periphery at any party where alcoholic drinks are being absorbed to excess, and you will see that alcohol dulls the inhibitions. As the night progresses, so the chatter increases, with the pitch of the laughter always rising in intensity.

Alcohol is a prime "tongue loosener." If you want someone to "spill the beans," just let him loose with a few pints of beer, and his tongue will invariable wag before very long.

Do you think alcohol is the cause of most major road accidents?

The statistics indicate that alcohol plays a major part in the majority of road fatalities, and indeed in most accidents. Grossly impaired judgment, reduced reflex activity, and reduced visual perception all play their part.

The "breathalyzer" test now in operation in some states in this country and in many other parts of the world is at least a stimulus for drinkers to refrain from driving.

It is believed that the use of breathalyzer machines by alert police officers may ultimately play a part in reducing the overall road toll.

Indeed, journals of the world are quite open when it comes to reporting opinions, facts, and figures on the road toll and its relation to alcohol.

Here is one, for example:

"The number of alcoholics in this country [U.S.] has increased from 6.5 million in the late 1960s to 9 million, according to the National Institute on Alcohol Abuse and Alcoholism.

"About 100,000 drinkers cross the road into alcoholism each year. . . . Half of the nation's 55,000 annual traffic deaths involve alcohol, and alcoholics figure in half the homicides and a third of the suicides in this country."[9]

A 1974 report indicates that the percentage of American adults who drink alcoholic beverages is at its highest point in 35 years. A gallup poll found that 68 percent of adults said they used alcoholic beverages, and 32 percent said they did not. Estimates show that the increase in drinkers from 1939 to 1974 has been more than twice as great among women—16 percentage points—as among men—7 percentage points.

These figures are quoted merely to give an indication of the widespread nature of addiction to alcohol in the community in general and to show some of the hazardous social and civic drawbacks that it presents.

What, then, is the answer for our young readers?

Unquestionably the only astute move is not to take that first fateful glass.

Let your friends (if friends such people could be termed) call you what they like. Shunning a new habit in youth is far simpler, less costly, less mentally traumatizing than trying later to eradicate a full-fledged addiction.

Once more I make it quite clear that I do not condone the social habit of drinking alcoholic liquor in any form. I shun it essentially for health reasons and also for moral considerations.

I hope our readers will do likewise. I guarantee it will be to their eternal welfare and better and happier living.

REFERENCES:
1. *Good Health,* November 1971.
2. *Medical Journal of Australia,* December 18, 1971, p. 1261.
3. *Facts on File,* 1974, p. 10.
4. *Documenta Giegy:* "Acceptable Addictions," 1971.
5. *British Medical Journal,* October 9, 1971.
6. *Ibid.*
7. *Medical Journal of Australia,* January 16, 1971.
8. *Documenta Giegy.*
9. *Listen,* February 1975, p. 21.

17

Artificial Sex

These days we often hear mention of words like "masturbation," "homosexuality," and "lesbianism." Not long ago they were whispered about in secret. But that is no longer so. Just the same, I'm sure lots of our youthful readers are not really clear as to what these words mean and what their significance is.

I agree. In fact, I've heard these words (and many associated ones) crop up. The way they are used convinces me that the person using the word is not really sure what he or she is talking about.

Masturbation

Let's start with masturbation.

This simply means the act of achieving sensuous gratification from artificial stimulation of the sex organs.

Is this a strictly male affair, or does it involve females as well?

It may be carried out by either males or females. In males it involves stimulation of the head of the penis, which is filled with millions of sensitive nerves. This rapidly produces an erection, and in a short time a surging sensation similar to the "orgasm" that climaxes sexual intercourse. At this juncture, seminal fluid pours forth from the end of the penis. Soon after this the erection subsides, and the affair is all over.

What about the female counterpart of this?

The action is not clear-cut in many cases, although in others there is a very definite end point, almost as marked as with the male.

What is involved?

As we've explained earlier, the part of major sensitivity in the female is the little organ called the clitoris. This is located just above the vaginal entrance. It can be stimulated by hand to produce an orgasm.

There are innumerable methods that have been used by young women over the years. In fact, one author wrote a book about it, so vast is the range of information!

At what age does masturbation start in both sexes?

It is believed that it begins at a very early age, really in infancy. Babies and small children soon discover that it is "fun" to "play with themselves" (as it is often described by parents).

Many authorities claim that every living soul has indulged in masturbation in some form or other (whether knowingly or not).

What about masturbation in adult life? Is it widely practiced?

Many researchers believe that the habit is transitory and is practiced mainly by the younger age group. It is often practiced for a short period of time, and then discontinued as the individual becomes older. Often, when marriage takes place, the normal form of sexual union replaces the artificial form of masturbation. Nevertheless, other researchers and experts claim that the habit does infiltrate the years of marriage and is widely practiced, by both males and females. I am sure "artificial sex" was never intended.

Is this form of activity physically harmful to the person indulging in it?

This question cannot be answered with certainty. Definite proof is lacking, and little research has been done. The fact remains that it is unnatural and that it fosters an undue preoccupation with sex.

Would you say that some of the bad results attributed to the habit are really fairly normal manifestations of the particular age group anyhow?

Oh, for sure. Girls in their teens are acutely aware of the possible range of "problems" that normally occur. Weight problems (too fat, too thin, too lanky, too spindly, too much bosom, not enough bosom); pimples; lack of grace and poise in women; slight build, lack of the usual "secondary sexual characteristics" in the male (muscular development, facial and underarm hair, and so on) occur on a never-ending basis. We have already talked about these. Now, these cannot be accounted for by the practice of "evil habits." They are just part of "growing up." Some young people mature early; others take a greater length of time.

Don't you think there is often a feeling of guilt associated with this action, just the same?

Yes. Quite often this dates back to babyhood when parents admonished their children on such habits, or found them in the process of genital stimulation, and either punished them or verbally criticized them for their "evil actions."

It doesn't take long for guilt complexes to become firmly fixed in a child's mind. Once there, they will remain for the rest of the lifetime.

As we said earlier, program something into the body's built-in computer system's memory bank, and it is there for all time. The same applies to this aspect of living too.

I've heard that the habit can possibly damage some of the glands of the body. Is this true, or is it just another one of those tales that get around?

We're not sure. It is well-known that prostatic enlargement is a very common disorder in males as they grow older.

Indeed, prostatic hypertrophy is extremely widespread in the male community. The prostate, if you recall our earlier discussions (and those pictures of the male reproductive organs) is a smallish gland located just below the bladder. Through it passes the urethra, the small tube that conveys urine from the bladder storehouse to the exterior. As the prostate increases in size, the prostate presses upward into the bladder, reducing both the capacity of that organ and the diameter of the urethra that passes through it. This can cause problems and frequently leads on to the need for surgical intervention.

Besides this, the prostate is a fairly common seat for cancer in older males. This serious condition usually commences as a simple hypertrophy or enlargement.

Some doctors believe that masturbation practiced regularly can predispose to early (and more severe) prostatic hypertrophy, with its attendant risks and discomforts.

Therefore there seems at least one major point in favor of nonindulgence in the habit?

Agreed. Whether the concept is true or not, we'll probably never know. But why play with fire (long-term)? In my set of books it's better to play it cool and not run any risks.

But wouldn't you say the immediate drawbacks would also be a factor against the habit?

Certainly. By experiencing these transient "pleasures" (if they can be called by this name, and even this is doubtful), it is very easy to develop a sex-orientated outlook. Indeed, the more the habit is practiced, the greater amounts of time will be spent in periods of erotic thought.

Nothing else will disturb a person's line of normal thought more than having his mind filled with sexually oriented material. If the mental computer is geared to fit this line of thought, he or she will gradually develop an impure, immoral outlook on life.

The well-known proverb, "As he thinketh in his heart, so is he," is certainly true. Fill the mind with impure thoughts, and that's the person one will inevitably become. You cannot miss. Indeed, so preoccupied with sensuous thoughts do some young folk become that their studies gradually start to fall behind. Their powers of normal concentration dwindle. Their entire outlook, their entire waking hours, can easily be filled with impure thoughts of the other sex.

For students trying to make the grade, trying to achieve an education that will fit them for a decent position in the world, this is a most unsatisfactory position to be in. I believe that sexually oriented activities must be reserved for after marriage. When carried out on a mutual basis, with a basic love for the partner, sex means so much. Carried out in a carnal, erratically emotional capacity, it misses out. Save it for when it means most to you and your marriage partner.

Many doctors also believe that the constant stimulation of artificial sex play can reduce the sensitivity of the nerve end organs located in the glans and clitoris. This, they say, can reduce the pleasure that sex will ultimately have in store for them. Perhaps this is an added reason why abstinence is best.

What is the situation with females?

Here it is simply to stimulate the clitoris to the point where orgasm occurs. It may be carried out in a multiplicity of ways. But the net result is the same. A very pleasurable sensation takes place. But once again, this is purely transitory. There is no warmth, no affection, no intrinsic love involved. It is a means to an end, and in this respect it has a lot in common with the drug addict who is merely interested in the next "fix" for his personal gratification.

Girls who become involved in continually practicing masturbation likewise tend to become preoccupied with sex. Eroticism fills their minds, often to the exclusion of the important facets of life.

There is more to youthful living than self-abuse. Leave sex to the time when complete, normal, natural fulfillment is within your grasp. Then it will mean so much more to you. One of the greatest things in life is the ability to share.

In this respect, sex represents the ultimate. Sharing oneself with another, giving oneself to a person with whom you are deeply involved emotionally, in the full sense of the word, represents the maximum in true love. That comes after marriage. Of this there is no doubt.

Lesbianism

Can we now leave this topic and get on to the other aspect of "artificial sex"? I refer to the topics of homosexuality and lesbianism. These may not be the most attractive subjects to discuss either, but I feel it's essential for our readers to have at least a passing knowledge of them, for both are rampant in the world today.

I agree that it's better to be armed with some knowledge about topics such as these. Sooner or later most of our readers will come across these facets of life in one form or another.

Tell us more about lesbianism.

This term refers to the relationship between two females who are sexually attracted to each other. It may occur in almost any age bracket, and often marital state is not necessarily a bar. Some females simply do not enjoy male company. They find members of their own sex far more pleasant to deal with, and they enjoy an erotic relationship with them.

A couple may carry on a clandestine relationship, just as illicitsexual relationships occur between unmarried boy-girl friendships. Frequently, especially in younger women, the precipitating trigger mechanism may have been an unsatisfactory affair with a male. The girl may have become jilted, or "used," or may have met with some other unfortunate incidents that turned her off the male sex very strongly. Often at this point, probably a sympathetic, understanding female associate befriended her, and so a different, unwholesome homosexual relationship gradually evolved.

In an older woman, marriage and reproduction may have taken place. She may finally have found sex in the normal sense unpleasant, "vulgar," "painful," or any of the other multitude of ways in which such people describe normal sexual relations. Bit by bit she finds herself attracted to another female who is usually able to administer affection, display feeling, kindness, tenderness, and sympathy. So another abnormal relationship begins and flourishes.

Of course, what many people cannot understand is how two women could possibly indulge in "sex" as we understand it.

The answer is, they cannot. Their actions are usually confined to the physical stimulation of each other's external genital organs.

Of course there are all manner of side issues connected with this. In some instances, there is a dominant personality. This partner tends to assume the "male" role in the relationship, and the lesser person the female role.

Some couples go to extreme lengths in their attachments. At times they will permanently live together. The dominant one will be the breadwinner and go out to work regularly, while the partner remains at home and carries out the usual domestic chores.

Male Homosexuality

What is the situation about male homosexuality?

Basically, this is very similar. It involves males that find other males more attractive sexually than females.

Of course, having a more varied anatomy, the schemes they can conjure up are more devious than those of their female counterpart. These vary all the way from mutual masturbation either simultaneously or in sequence, to forms of simulated intercourse which to normal people are abhorrent and repulsive.

The ultimate objective, irrespective of the method employed, is to reach an orgasmic climax. This is the highlight of the exercise.

How is homosexuality regarded in the community?

In some countries it has been legalized between consenting adult male partners. However, most heterosexually inclined people regard homosexual activities with a very definite contempt. Moreover the number of factors militating against the practice are enough to make aspirants and condoners hate it.

What are some of these?

Perhaps the most outstanding aspect is that it's entirely immoral in a so-called Christian society. The Scriptures frequently speak out in crystal-clear tones against the practice. Indeed, at least one city was destroyed because its inhabitants practiced the vile habit. God rained down fire and brimstone on the city of Sodom to cleanse the spot from its foulness and wickedness. The word "sodomy" remains in our current vocabulary to this day as a memorial to their wickedness and sinful ways.

Many Bible students also believe that this was one reason why God poured down the great Flood. It was to re-create the world, a better, purer place for man to live in. The degree of willful sin occurring in the days just prior to Noah's great triumph was of the most degrading nature.

But these are really moral issues. Although I go along with them entirely, do you have supportive evidence that homosexuality as such is an adverse practice in the community?

Certainly. It is very well documented that venereal disease is rampant among people practicing it. Indeed, homosexuals are an important reason for the sudden upsurge of VD in the postwar era. In fact, some of the other more serious (but less frequent) forms of VD are readily transmitted by this class of person, the experts tell us.

Do you feel that we tend to criticize this type of person a bit unjustly? After all, we probably consider that we are "normal" and they are "abnormal," when they probably believe the reverse.

This could be so. As it happens, an increasing number of doctors, psychiatrists, and social workers believe that homosexuals are in need of specialized treatment. They believe that they suffer from some inherent defect. They feel that these unfortunates should receive remedial treatment just as mental defects are treated these days. After all, it is not so very long ago that anyone with a psychiatric illness was considered insane and promptly shut up in an asylum and given scant attention. These days he is admitted to a psychiatric center for proper assessment, tests, and therapy. Times have changed. Maybe this is how we should be attending to the homosexual misfit in the community.

It is probable that times will change. But this doesn't alter the fact that God specifically states His objection to these people as a type.

The sooner widespread efforts are made to help them adjust back to normality the better. In this way mankind will be doing a service to his fellowman. Simultaneously he will be bringing those that have fallen by the wayside to a better understanding of what true, normal living entails. What better and more satisfying work could there be for some types of social worker? We hope to see it occur in the not-too-distant future.

Diseases That Come if
You Play With Fire

We've gone into quite a bit of detail on physiology, anatomy, sex, reproduction, and related topics. How about our taking a look at some of the abnormalities? We could discuss some of the sexually transmitted diseases.

That is a good suggestion. The disorders you mention are collectively called venereal diseases (VD). In ancient mythology Venus was the goddess of love. "Venereal" is related to Venus and the lovemaking process!

Is this merely one disease, or are there several?

There are quite a few. However, the two commonest ones are known as gonorrhea and syphilis.

We sometimes hear about "nonspecific urethritis," "chanchroid," and "lymphogranuloma venereum," but from a practical point of view these are not nearly so common or important (although they can be serious if contracted).

Gonorrhea

Is gonorrhea very common?

It is extremely common, although at one stage we nearly had the disease beaten. But general indifference, changing patterns of behavior in our wildly "swinging" world, and the permissive era have all contributed to a violent upsurge which is little short of alarming. In fact, the World Health Organization estimates that 100 million new cases of gonorrhea occur each year. It is now one of the most common communicable diseases. However, for every reported case there are perhaps ten that are not reported. This gives some idea of the enormity of the present problem. Usually about five times as many males are reported as females.

What are the symptoms?

There is *always* a history of sexual intercourse. About four to ten days after, there may be discomfort when passing urine. There may be a thick vaginal discharge. Sometimes there is low pelvic discomfort and a fever. However, in mild cases there may be very few (if any) symptoms at all.

In the male, there is burning and discomfort with urination. Invariably a thick, yellowish discharge occurs. There may be local discomfort and perhaps a fever.

Confirmation and Treatment

How is diagnosis confirmed?

The doctor usually orders a pathology test. The germ can clearly be seen sitting inside the affected cells. The germs are known by the technical name *Neisseria gonorrhoeae,* and under the microscope they are seen as "gram-negative intracellular diplococci." Finding the organism is diagnostic, although the symptoms themselves are usually adequate evidence on which to start intensive treatment.

What does the doctor do?

He commences intensive antibiotic treatment. Although penicillin was initially the drug of first choice (and one single injection usually cleared it within hours), this is not the present situation. Resistant cases are common. Sometimes special cultures and sensitivity tests are carried out, and the best drug is determined on the results of the tests.

One thing is imperative. Treatment must be continued until a complete cure has been effected.

Is sexual intercourse the only way in which the disease can be contracted?

For all practical purposes, yes. The organism soon dies outside of the human body. There is little chance of "picking it up from seats in public toilets" and other places (as lots of suffering patients fondly try to have one believe).

Syphilis

What about syphilis?

This is fast getting out of hand too. Like gonorrhea, with the advent of the antibiotics and soon after World War II, the disease showed a dramatic decline. Indeed, it looked as if its days were numbered. But for reasons identical with gonorrhea, syphilis has rapidly climbed the popularity polls once more.

"World-wide incidence of syphilis has increased by 90 percent over the past ten years—approximately twenty million people are now thought to be infected," reports the *Medical Journal of Australia*.[1]

What are the symptoms of syphilis?

One to eight weeks after infection a small sore (chancre) develops on the external genitals—the penis in the male, and the labia in the female. Sometimes the lymph glands in the groin swell and become tender. However, as if by magic, and with no treatment whatsoever, this sore will disappear. But a few weeks later, a generalized body rash will manifest itself.

This is called secondary syphilis.

But the really serious situation arises anywhere from two to twenty years after all this has quietly settled. The syphilis germ (an organism corkscrew in shape and named *Treponema pallidum*) smolders on beneath the surface.

Gradually, quietly, insidiously it is carrying out its death-dealing work like a sinister underground movement. This is the latent stage. Finally, tertiary syphilis breaks out. This can affect almost any organ in the body. The eyes, blood vessels, brain, bones, skin, hard and soft tissues alike, can fall prey to its savage ravages. Heart disease used to be a common manifestation, and the terrible aortic aneurysms (now rarely seen, fortunately) could reach massive sizes before suddenly bursting and causing instant death. If infection is located in the brain, gradual destruction of that organ occurs too.

Treatment and Advice

How about treatment–is this satisfactory?

Once diagnosis has been made (and special and accurate tests are freely available for this), intensive therapy will yield good results. But the emphasis is on early diagnosis.

Aren't there certain legal entanglements associated with these diseases?

Yes. In most countries of the world the governments take an intense interest in the disease. Realizing the tremendous speed with which they can spread, and the disastrous consequences they can have (both in the short and long term), it is now legally mandatory in most civilized countries to be treated until cured.

To make it simple for possible victims, there are government clinics in most cities that will diagnose and treat the disorders free of charge.

How can a person be assured of not contracting these terrible diseases?

There is one sure and certain method. Maintain a high moral code, and there is little to worry about. The diseases are transmitted solely by sexual intercourse with an infected person. Therefore, not playing around with sex before marriage is the best advice I can offer.

The most likely persons having VD are those who freely "sleep around." Of course, after marriage, when you have only one partner, there is no likelihood whatsoever of either person contracting the disease if each is faithful to the other. VD will not become a problem unless you personally allow it. It's up to you!

REFERENCE:
1. "Medical Journal of Australia," October 24, 1970.

Parting Words

Here we are at the final chapter of our book.

The time has sped by at an amazing pace! Maybe that's because we've been such an interested trio.

Trio?

Yes. You and me and our reader.

I wonder if we'll ever discover who some of our unknown friends are!

I'm not sure, but I hope so. Our address will be clearly printed in the front of this little volume. We'd be delighted to hear from any reader who would care to write to us. After all, we are real live people. We're not merely a name printed on the front cover. It would be a real delight if anyone should write. And most probably we would drop them a note in reply.

Would you care to tell our friends about the "other book"?

Most certainly. This book of course, has been written essentially for teen-age girls. Just in case there are teen-age boys in your family, or if you happen to have a teen-age boyfriend you think would benefit by some extra reading, we've also prepared a companion book entitled, "What a

Young Man Should Know About Sex.'' It is printed and published by the same company that prints this book. Mail inquiries will be promptly attended to.

Incidentally, books often make welcome birthday and Christmas gifts too. Some families will wish to buy the two volumes at the same time—particularly those with growing families. It's a good idea to have one for the boys and one for the girls; and separate copies are readily available.

Do you have any final thoughts to offer our reader before we say good-bye?

I'd like to suggest that you give thoughtful consideration to the ideas we've offered in this book. In the future, if you have some spare moments, why not flick back over some of the chapters. Indeed, you will find material that could suit nearly every day of your life. You will notice that nearly every chapter is self-contained, so you can start anywhere you like.

Glance through the table of contents at the front, and this will give you a quick guide as to where any particular information you desire can be located.

Many problems occur in life. But they can *all* be solved. The method may not be obvious at the moment, but if the clear-cut principles outlined are followed, I am sure you will find an answer.

Just remember that life will be much happier, much less complicated, if you keep physically and mentally fit. This is imperative. There is no fun in being ill. Sticking to simple principles, you can stay healthy and vigorous at all times.

Set your goals in life at an early stage. Set lots of minor goals. Bear these well in mind. Once your course has been set, make every effort to stick to it. This way, you will succeed beyond your wildest dreams.

Keep in touch with the Supreme Intelligence at all times. Make a point of taking God into partnership in your activities.

Don't think you are being odd or childish or foolish in doing this. Actually, you are being sensible. God promises to help those who call upon Him in time of need. Better to call on Him often; then you will receive much help as you journey through life.

Don't get carried away with some of the foolish, popular pastimes of the world. Enjoy life, for sure; but don't become ensnared in the traps we've outlined.

Although they may momentarily appear attractive, so many long-term problems can loom. It's not worth the risks involved.

Be a stalwart. Resist temptation. Keep a level head. Don't give in. This is how character is built.

In today's world a person with character is someone to whom people can look up. It is something worth striving to achieve. These are the people the world is seeking. These are the leaders and decision makers of tomorrow. Weaklings who give in at the slightest pretext are not worth their salt. Their value in life is negligible.

People of stamina, of personal fortitude and courage, are the ones the world seeks out and in due course will honor. Never forget it.

We wish you every success and much happiness as you journey through life.

Keep your feet firmly on the ground. Keep one hand in touch with God, and your life will be happy and full of meaning; success unlimited will come your way. Of that there is no doubt.

Good-bye and good wishes.